# Mini Farming for Beginners

**The Ultimate Guide to Remaking Your Backyard Into a Mini Farm and Creating a Self-Sustaining Organic Garden**

**Brenda Sanders**

© Copyright All rights reserved.

This eBook is provided with the sole purpose of providing relevant information on a specific topic for which every reasonable effort has been made to ensure that it is both accurate and reasonable. Nevertheless, by purchasing this eBook, you consent to the fact that the author, as well as the publisher, are in no way experts on the topics contained herein, regardless of any claims as such that may be made within. As such, any suggestions or recommendations that are made within are done so purely for entertainment value. It is recommended that you always consult a professional prior to undertaking any of the advice or techniques discussed within.

This is a legally binding declaration that is considered both valid and fair by both the Committee of Publishers Association and the American Bar Association and should be considered as legally binding within the United States.

The reproduction, transmission, and duplication of any of the content found herein, including any specific or extended information, will be done as an illegal act regardless of the end form the information ultimately takes. This includes copied versions of the work, both physical, digital, and audio unless express consent of the Publisher is provided beforehand. Any additional rights reserved.

Furthermore, the information that can be found within the pages described forthwith shall be considered both accurate and truthful when it comes to the recounting of facts. As such, any use, correct or incorrect, of the provided information will render the Publisher free of responsibility as to the actions taken outside of their direct purview. Regardless, there are zero scenarios where the original author or the Publisher can be deemed liable in any fashion for any damages or hardships that may result from any of the information discussed herein.

Additionally, the information in the following pages is intended only for informational purposes and should thus be thought of as universal. As befitting its nature, it is presented without assurance regarding its prolonged validity or interim quality. Trademarks that are mentioned are done without written consent and can in no way be considered an endorsement from the trademark holder.

## Introduction

Home food production is an important skill, that makes positive contributions to the family's physical and financial health. At the same time, it re-establishes our connection with the roots of our ancestors by reaffirming our connection to nature and natural laws, and provides a sense of ability by ensuring the supply of basic necessities (food), thus playing an important psychological and spiritual role effect. It is also important that, for a variety of reasons, the quality of food produced by households is superior to that provided by supermarkets. Commercial demand has driven many factors to reduce the nutritional value of commercial food. Since almost no food is produced during use, the fruit and vegetable varieties are selected according to the suitability of machine picking, long-distance transportation and refrigeration, so that they still look good when entering the supermarket.

This results in a uniform appearance, products with attractive appearance that look better than their taste, and nutritional value is much lower than similar products produced locally. Spinach is a good example. With proper care and refrigeration, fresh spinach can deteriorate for three weeks or more. However, even at 39 degrees in the dark, it can only lose about half of the B vitamins in a week. Therefore, in a brightly lit refrigerator in a supermarket, the attractive baby spinach bags actually have fewer nutrients than their own spinach that turns white and frozen on the day of harvest. The same situation applies to other fruits and vegetables.

Considering the time it takes for packaging, transportation and storage, home-grown products that are quickly canned, frozen or dehydrated after harvest will pack more nutritious food than so-called fresh products in supermarkets. Nutritional density is not the only factor promoting household food production. Pesticide residues are another important consideration. The company's farms and orchards use a variety of pesticides to protect the quantity and appearance of their harvest. According to a 1999 report by the US Government's Consumer Alllance, "Apples grown in the US usually contain four pesticides, and

There are as many as 10 residues. The same report lists several common vegetables, including butternut squash and spinach, which often contain multiple pesticide residues, some as many as 14 residues. The report also cited data indicating widespread use of illegal pesticides and the continued existence of carcinogenic chemicals It was banned in today's corporate harvest decades ago. In addition, small home gardens are ideal for using organic or semi-organic materials and methods, which can significantly reduce or even eliminate the need for synthetic pesticides.

In any case, if the family gardener decides to use the over-the-counter pesticides that are usually available, the gardener personally ensures proper use and schedules to ensure that the amount of residues in the food is far less than typical commercial planted products. Excellent taste is the main benefit of home-made food. The two main factors that affect taste are freshness and the variety actually planted. With the backyard garden, vine-treated tomatoes can be served within minutes of picking eggplants from the vines, while supermarket tomatoes are harvested when they are green and mature during transportation. For any kind of food store, it is impossible to exceed the freshness in the backyard garden.

In addition, due to the selection of vegetable varieties used in corporate agriculture (also known as "agricultural integrated enterprises"), because they have the advantages of transportation toughness, mature and easy mechanical harvesting, some of the most delicious varieties of fruits and vegetables are even It is not available in the United States. Supermarkets because they are not very suitable for mechanical picking or scraping. On the contrary, family gardeners are free to choose thousands of common and / or heirloom varieties according to their personal preferences. Commercial growers do business.

Therefore, the US dollar is its value standard. Your health (even beyond their minds) is a secondary issue. Their main goal is Produce goods at the lowest cost, sell them at the highest price, and get the most profit. This process does not automatically bring evil, but it is obvious that you can invest a lot of energy to ensure that the food is safe, delicious, and healthy, which is far more than a company on half a continent. Finally, the economy is an important reason for producing and preserving food at home. The mini-agricultural production method described in this book only produces fresh agricultural products, and only accounts for the percentage of the cost of purchasing similar food in supermarkets. This means that growing your own food can add valuable funds to your family's budget, while keeping your own food can guarantee healthy food during periods of barrenness.

It is conceivable that the use of intensive technology to transform from vegetable gardening to large-scale micro-agriculture can provide more than 80% of the food for households and reduce the cash requirement by thousands of dollars each year. I have met many people who have planted gardens but have since given up planting. Although the details are different, in all these cases, the former gardener has encountered unrealistic or unrealistic goals. Many people move to houses with small courtyards, so traditional gardens are not suitable. Some people are injured causing mobility problems. Others encountered problems with harmful insects or other pests.

In the end, many people just gave up because gardening takes too much time and trouble compared to gardening. The lesson I learned is that people need to have reasonable prospects to achieve their gardening goals, otherwise they wo n't bother. The goal of the miniature farmer is similar to that of the family gardener, but more emphasis is placed on economy. The purpose of micro-farmers is to reduce the income needed by providing most of the household's food needs. This can enable parents to stay at home with their children, make it possible to go to school at home, improve living conditions under fixed income conditions, or act as a buffer against uncertain economic conditions.

In the following chapters, I intend to demonstrate how to achieve the goals of gardening and small farming. Although any obstacles may be encountered, how to come with more fun and less time, energy, money and equipment than you expected achieve. The methods used in this book are a combination of traditional methods, biodynamic methods, bio-intensive growth methods, French intensive methods, square feet methods, and other methods using elevated beds, which I call "intensive agriculture". It stands on the shoulders of many great, dedicated gardeners, thinkers, philosophers, and farmers, so I have no special praise for it, but it is synthesized based on my own experience, hoping to save the reader a lot of trial and try. error.

The contents of this book can be used at all levels. It can be used for efficient amateur gardening to improve nutrition and enjoyment, more devoted to gardening, and perfect mini farming. Therefore, my goal is to help readers start to develop more economical, nutritious and safe food with minimal effort, and at the same time help readers reconnect with the natural and heritage cycle in a spirit-enhancing manner.

## Chapter One
## What is mini farming

Mini-farming ensures that whatever is farmed, raised and grown on the field is eaten by the farmers themselves. They live off the soil and have all the food they need for their own consumption. In other words, they are fairly self-sufficient when it comes to what they eat. You can also also learn that sustainable farming and self-sufficient farming are used interchangeably because they are one and the same. The size of the land they own is generally, but not always relatively small, compared to the more economically driven farmers. You can also find such small farms referred to as mini-farms or micro-farms.

Commercial farming, on the other hand, is where crops are grown and cattle are raised for others to make some income. Not because farming is a profitable, well-to-do business, it is not, but by becoming a small farmer on one farm with the goal of making a well-known market, understanding what the existing prices are for their crops and livestock, and what the niche market can offer to them income, both now and in the future.

## The principle of mini-farming

The core theory of mini-farming-land management: First and foremost, as has already been stated, there is no need for a big piece of land to become self-sufficient. So how small is it? Okay, on one acre of land, one can potentially become self-sufficient very happily. One acre of land can be used for small-scale farming on mini-farms that are very happily self-sufficient. However, since self-sufficiency can be exercised on mini-farms, land conservation is essential. It will then become the most critical concept for sustainable farming and the development of your mini farm.

The hint, of course, is, in the very word, sustainable meaning to keep things running. If the land you use to cultivate is not maintained correctly, you will never be able to maintain any crops or livestock at an reasonable degree of productivity. This covers both large-scale and small-scale farming. Mismanagement is going to give you the same outcome. What you will end up with will be both alive and stable plants and livestock, and your aspirations for self-sufficiency will be unfulfilled.

In running a micro farm or a small farm, there needs to be a balance between the animals and the plants, because hopefully, you want to build a food chain where they feed each other. You need manure from farm animals to enrich the soil so that the soil can then grow healthy crops and, in effect, go back to feed the livestock.

There is a need for crop rotation with small-scale farming on mini-farms for sustainability. It is difficult to cultivate crops on the same piece of land year after year. Crops dress like this and quickly succumb to illness. However, the issue does not end here, because what happens is that the disease agents that invade the plant grow to such an degree that the disease ultimately becomes uncontrollable. So prepare your small farm carefully, and make sure that every portion of the land is held bare so that you can execute your crop rotation programme.

## Why you should take up mini farming

Most people no longer want to be part of a growing mob that demands more and more. And some, also want to see how they're capable of surviving without the need to hit a supermarket of anything readily accessible. Whereas other people are only living in their houses as a means to lead a healthy ecological life.

If you are mentioned in the above article, it might be time for you to start setting up your own mini farm. It may sound overwhelming, but you can do it right where you are! All you need is foresight, inspiration to learn new things, and a strategy! I have a fantastic set of worksheets to support you with the preparation component, and they're available at the end of this post.

Save Money

The main reason people are turning to live off the land is because of income. Living paycheque to paycheque is no fun unless there's more than money left to spare. As the cost of living continues to rise, money is a problem for a lot of people. Not to mention, it reflects heat, consumerism, and, to a degree, greed.

Through raising your own food in your own yard, you're avoiding the need to pay for grocery shopping every week. When making your own clothing, there's no need to scour the internet for the newest fashion trends from brands vying for your attention. The savings you would achieve from slowly being self-sufficient with your mini farm in tow will have a positive effect on your financial life.

Learn New Skills

As you learn to take responsibility and evolve individually and do what you need to live, you can, of course, develop a lot of new experience and skills. If you are planning a scheme to develop your own well and provide a water supply to your property with the aid of a water pressure booster system. Or to measure the acidity of the soil and determine when different seeds should be planted. Through living off the ground, you will build up a never-ending supply of wisdom that contributes to a great sense of fulfillment.

Learning new skills is a wonderful aim that can go a long way towards developing your own mini farm. My "Jump Start to Homestead Preparation" worksheets will help you get your plans out of your mind, into some paper, and into a doable plan. It's in my tool list, and at the end of this article you will get a password for it!

Stress Busting

You may be feeling that this term undermines the concept of making your own property. Yeah, some aspects of being self-sufficient can be difficult, but the ultimate drinking up of fresh oxygen every day, being in the midst of greenery and doing something you love, would cause your well-being to flourish. Let's not say, actually going outside is confirmed by evidence that decreases blood pressure and boosts short-term memory.

Natural Foods

Pesticides and artificial fertilizers used by different producers and corporations to make food crops grow faster are another explanation why people choose to eat their own organic food. We seem to be very oblivious to the fact that any piece of food we pick in the store has gone on a journey.

We prefer to drink food, whether good or wrong, with no understanding of whether it has been drenched in toxins or, in the case of animals, it has been handled and fed poorly during its lifespan. You're in charge of the trip with your own mini-farm. From eggs to carrots, at least you know exactly how he's been looked after all his life and how you think he's safe enough to feed.

## Simple tricks to maximize your space

Many of us look forward to the unmistakable taste of fresh, locally grown vegetables and fruit, particularly those coming from our own soil. Don't despair of those of you who would like to grow food at home but have limited space. Your vision of home-grown food is still within your grasp.

You might be curious how to grow vegetables if you have little to no room with full sun exposure, but certain vegetables can tolerate partial shade, and some may also be called 'shaded vegetables' because they won't tolerate full sun exposure.

You may live in an apartment with not much more than a balcony, but you love fresh veggies and would still like to grow your own-no problem 1.) Container planting If you have little outdoor space, be it a small yard, a shared courtyard or a balcony, a garden container with vegetables and fruit may be the perfect place for you.

One of the best things about container gardening is the potential to grow almost any vegetable and several varieties of fruit, provided the right conditions and enough space for an suitable container.

With the correct amount of sun exposure and watering method, it is also possible to raise small fruit trees or bushes successfully in this manner. In my day, I saw both lemon trees and blueberry bushes grow in overground planters-what a delicious way to fill your container garden with color!

Container gardens are also incredibly space-efficient, because any ounce of soil in your container will count for fruit and vegetable production-no growing area will be lost while you take care of and harvest your plants.

Container garden also has the additional advantage of being a perfect backsaver, or it can be adapted for those with limited mobility, making sure that growing fresh fruit and vegetables at home is available to everyone.

Another interesting thing about container gardening is the opportunity as a gardener to follow the heat, if appropriate, because containers can be moved during the day. If you don't have time to push containers when life keeps on around you, there's no trouble planting the amount of sun you have.

Although it is true that many plants would need a minimum of 6 hours of direct sunshine a day, there are a variety of shade vegetables that can survive or grow in partial shade and dappled sunlight.

A few things to remember when gardening containers: 'Upcycling' will lead to some really fascinating containers-steel pasta strainers are perfect for kitchen herbs, recycled antique boxes add charm to your vegetative designs and even up-cycled plastic totes will make fantastic planters if you're more concerned about functionality than appearance. You're confined to your creativity and tastes. You'll want to remember to require drainage, so if appropriate, drill holes or otherwise puncture the bottom of your selected containers. We've also found a fantastic lightweight and durable fabric elevated planter that we've been able to bring to home here-and we're on our second season. It makes growing vegetables easy for both young and old!

Almost every plant can thrive in a container provided the container is big enough.

Straw bales themselves can be used as planting bins, even though they can be a little messy and break down fairly easily, they are a viable choice. We've loved pumpkins and zucchini right off the top of the straw bales this season-and it couldn't be simpler (see how this is achieved here.) Make careful to have ample water and food while planting in containers, because soil in containers can dry quicker and nutrients continue to flow into them quicker than their in-ground counterparts.

Assess the exposure to the sun and grow accordingly.

Vertical planting: Well, vertical planting. There are so many options to grow upward-let's face it, most vegetables and fruit bearing plants grow upward-when adapting food production to a smaller location, try using a conventional trellis to a recycled pallet planter to a hanging hydroponic window garden. The opportunities for vertical planting are extensive and require just a certain amount of creativity-making usable space out of wasted space is the secret to optimum productivity in the small urban garden.

-- edibles adapt themselves to vertical gardening you may be wondering; well, I'm happy to say that the list is long. Here are only a couple to get you started: tomatoes: cherry tomatoes in particular (but most varieties do) are very happy to grow upward, provided the right amount of encouragement. Old nylons cut into strips are perfect for connecting the plants to their upward systems because they are lightweight which can result in the least amount of tension on the plant where they are attached. Perhaps you're not wearing nylons, or your nylons are much too expensive to be used in your urban garden, don't worry, pick up some at the thrift shop, they're going to cost next to zero. Instead, cultivate at the top of the wall down to the cellar, and watch the branches flood with delicious cherry tomatoes as summer progresses.

Winter squash and melons: these plants emerge naturally in the direction of the sun. Again, they will require adequate care, particularly when they begin to bear fruit, but they respond well to being trained to where you have a room.

Peas and pole beans would happily grow something large enough to help them Cucumbers this favorite afternoon tea, spa or spritzer ingredient on the cooler days of summer is fairly easy to grow in the smallest of spaces.

Asian vegetables, salad greens, strawberries and kitchen herbs will all flourish happily in nothing more than a recycled pallet on its side. Instructions for this can be found here.

Greens, strawberries or kitchen herbs can also grow happily in parts of rain gutter that can either be hanged or placed on the side of almost every south facing structure or in a network of hanging bottles in the south facing window as seen here. Hanging rain gutter greenhouse directions are available here.

Potatoes, guy. Yup, even potatoes can expand vertically if they have the right container to do so. Imagine that you're using a sterile garbage can with all sorts of holes cut in the rim. Throw down a few inches of soil and compost, add the cut and cured bits of seed potatoes and cover with 6 more inches of earth. Wind. Wind. When the aerial portions of the plant have reached around 6-8 inches, apply more soil leaving just a few inches of green exposed soil. This cycle can be repeated a few times during the season. Once the plants turn brown and die, it's time to reap. The potatoes on the top would be smaller and more delicate than those on the bottom, just like the gourmet "fresh" potatoes sold at the supermarket at a premium price. I've read of vertical potatoes growing in a straw-filled container (rather than soil) that makes harvesting easier, and I'm hoping to try it this year. Stop Press: This worked well for us, so it seems that the potatoes are growing better, leading to a heavier harvest. I kept covering the straw with the gradually disintegrating straw bales in which our pumpkin and zuccini rise.

Try hanging planters: Strawberries will flourish in hanging containers, and even tomatoes will happily rise upside down from the bottom of a hanging bucket. Our field covering strawberries do nothing more than make fat, happy chipmunks, hanging them means you might eat any of them, too.

3.) Raised beds and square foot gardens: if your planting area is wide enough for raised beds, it can be a perfect way to optimize room and energy. Not only do raised beds support more plants per square foot, but planting in a raised bed also decreases the need for weeds. It also makes weeds much harder to dig out throughout the season, and can be a great relief to the back, and if the beds are well laid apart, then the wheelchair planting is a nice possibility in small spaces. Garden care has never been simpler.

Here are only a couple of the benefits of growing food in a raised bed in a small garden: a long growing season. A raised bed is going to warm up better than the field in the morning, and in the fall the bed will quickly be tempted to prolong the growing season by a couple weeks or so-this will yield in a smaller garden.

Place, place, place: grow food at the place of your choosing, regardless of soil conditions, while you apply your own.

Raised beds provide excellent drainage under all soil conditions, no matter where your garden is situated.

Soil compaction is no longer an problem, so managing and preserving soil and weeding would be much easier for smaller areas.

Each square inch of soil in your limited room must be expended on food growth, as none will be lost underfoot.

Depending about how high you want to create the raised beds in your small garden, you could totally eradicate the need to bend over. In the worst scenario, even though the raised beds are just a foot and a half high, you're not going to stretch too much.

Ideally, the raised bed is 18-24 inches tall, so if you create the raised beds on the top of the actual soil, you'll have some leeway here. I have been successfully gardening in boxes installed over the earth with just one foot of soil coverage.

Keyhole gardens Keyhole gardens are built to optimize space by reducing the need for walkways as seen in conventional row gardening or with raised beds. The architecture is also intended to be draught-resistant and to provide nutrients by compost during the growing season.

Keyhole gardens are a raised style bed that takes the rough form of a circle with a "keyhole" shaped path that provides access to the whole garden. There is a vertical tunnel in the middle of the pipe, which contains several layers of compost. When manure melts down, it provides nutrients and moisture to the surface. Certainly an effective way to expand, keyhole gardens can be designed with several different materials as a fast Google search for the word can prove. If you have a circular area of about 8-10 feet in diameter, you can use any suitable material that can be easily reached by corrugated siding, cedar poles, landscaping blocks, bricks or some combination thereof.

5.) Eatable nature, woodland gardens and permascaping The practice of edible permascaping includes planting seasonal food in places where ornamentals will typically take up space. In reality, many common ornamentals are edible, so transforming your landscape into a food-bearing paradise is simpler than it may seem.

When you look at your entire property as a possible land on which to grow crops, the ability to increase the yield increases accordingly. Lawns, for example, may quickly be turned into garden plots, flowering annual gardens can also contain plants that are both spectacular and nutritious, and even forested areas on your land may grow food (and in some situations may even have something wild worth harvesting).

Public gardens No south-facing window, deck or yard? Get a community garden, it's a perfect place to cultivate food while improving ties with neighbors. If there's no community garden in your neighborhood yet, might there be a vacant lot to launch one?

One thing is for sure, learning how to grow vegetables with those in your neighborhood and sharing ideas and tools would do more than just put food on the table. Collective planting, or even

even sharing planting, can help create and improve connections within your community.

A community garden is also a perfect way to give children access to food processing that they would not otherwise receive. In the future, we will face many problems in the area of natural resources and food production, and the ability to produce food in one way or another is a capability that will be very useful to future generations.

## Chapter Two
## Best plants for mini farming

### Lavender

Lavender can be found in just about everything, from food flavorings to drugs to fragrances. The essential oil is also among the most popular in a flourishing wellness environment.

### Bamboo

Bamboo is primarily sold as a potted plant or landscaping plant. What makes it especially competitive is its potential to expand very rapidly. Without a ton of space, you can generate a lot of stuff.

### Basil

Basil is a common herb used in loads of dishes. You can cultivate it quickly indoors or in a small container greenhouse. If you're going to grow it outdoors, it should flourish in dry, humid conditions. You would then supply it to food suppliers, retail shops or directly to customers on farmers' markets.

Cilantro

Cilantro is another common herb that doesn't take a lot of space to produce. In addition to its distinctive taste, it can also be used as a digestion aid, and it is popular with pharmaceutical companies that produce supplements.

Chives

Chives may be cultivated indoors or outdoors. And unlike many other herbs, they're pretty healthy. But you can grow them in nearly any environment in the U.S.

Ginseng

Ginseng is a very common grow in the health and wellness industry. It is used in a number of medications, vitamins and teas. It takes a while to get going. But once your crops have yielded, you should predict big revenues from strong global demand.

Gourmet Garlic

Garlic can be used in just about every sort of sauce. Yet standard garlic is very abundant and does not have a very high quality. However, there are a few animals that are considered "gourmet" because they are a little more rare. When you're able to spend in these early days, they will potentially pay off over time.

## Arugula

Arugula is a type of leafy green that gives a zippy flavor to salads or side dishes. It's really popular with trendy farm-to-table restaurants. Yet you might also sell it to safe customers on farmers' markets.

## Corn

Corn has long been one of the most popular crops in the world, especially in the Midwest. It takes a decent amount of space. So it can be used for anything from feed to fuel.

## Soybeans

Soybeans are very similar to corn in a variety of respects. They grow under common conditions and can be used in milk, feed and a number of other items.

## Wheat

Wheat is a common crop to be grown in the Great Plains. But you can also grow it on a small scale in a backyard or in a small row garden. It's pretty hardy, so there are several different varieties that can contribute to very high yields of grain.

## Sorghum

Sorghum is a type of grain sometimes used in syrups and beverages. It thrives in hot climates. It's good for any place that loves long summers. It's extremely common at the moment because of the rise of craft beer and home brewing hobbyists.

## Saffron

Saffron is a spice that comes from saffron crocus flowers, a purple-blue herb that thrives in sunny surroundings. You're going to need a decent amount of space, as each flower only produces a small amount of spice. But saffron has a relatively high price tag, making it a especially lucrative crop.

## Cherry Tomatoes

Cherry tomatoes are small and can grow quickly in the backyard or in a small garden. The tomatoes can be selected continuously during the season. And it's the right choice for farmers who want a steady crop yield.

Goji Berries

Goji berries are very popular at the moment because they are known as "superfoods." With a number of antioxidants and vitamins, they are popular in organic drinks, smoothies and bowls. We are also very versatile and able to survive in dry conditions.

Hostas

Hostas is a common plant used for landscaping and gardening. They're very hardy, and they can be quickly separated and distributed. Then you will consistently build more and market it to landscaping shops or directly to customers.

Arborvitae

Arborvitae is a type of small evergreen tree common in landscaping. They can be sold in small pots or in full-grown plants. You may even distribute it to build many more to market over time.

## Shiitake Mushrooms

Shiitakes and other gourmet mushrooms are very common in a variety of dishes, particularly in trendy restaurants and specialty food stores. They're also rising very quickly and taking relatively little attention.

## Flowers

If you have the room to start a flower garden or grow any flowering trees or shrubs, you may easily sell potted or cut flowers to local companies or directly to customers for benefit.

## Bonsai Plants

Bonsai trees are generally sold as small, potted plants. They're popular with collectors and homeowners looking for a unique décor. They do need very little space to expand.

## How mini farming works for you

Many households perform the task of gardening or small-scale farming as a hobby to get fresh-grown produce and potentially save money by purchasing food in the supermarket. Unfortunately, the most popular gardening approaches end up being so costly that even some passionate garden writers claim that gardening can at best be called a break-even affair. Looking at the most common methods of planting, these writers are totally right. Popular gardening methods are significantly more costly than required since they were initially developed to benefit from the economies of scale of corporate agribusiness.

When home gardeners attempt to use these techniques on a smaller scale, it's a success if they break even for a few years, so they're more likely to lose money. The prices of tillers, irrigation machines, large volumes of soil, transplants, bulbs, fertilizers and insecticides add up very rapidly. Balanced against the fact that most home gardeners only grow vegetables, and vegetables make up just less than 10% of the calories the average consumer eats, it soon becomes obvious that even if the cost of a vegetable garden is zero, the total amount of money invested in the food budget will be insignificant.

For example, if the gross economic value of vegetables harvested from the garden in a single season amounts to around $350 and vegetables could be provided free of charge, the economic gain would only be $7 a week if distributed over the year. The solution to this issue is to reduce prices and increase the profitability of the finished product. This can be done by growing your own seedlings from open-pollinated plant varieties so that you can conserve the seeds and prevent the expense of purchasing both transplants and seeds, using efficient planting methods that use less space, deliberately composting to minimize the need for fertilizers, and growing calorie-dense crops to have a higher proportion of the household's caloric intake.

Using this mix, the economic calculation would work in favour of the gardener instead of the garden supplies shop, so it is very possible to provide all the food of the family but the meat from a relatively small garden. According to the USDA, the total annual per capita food spending in 2001 was $2,964, with food prices rising at a rate of 27.7% over the previous 10 years.

Understanding that food is bought with post-tax dollars, it is clear that home farming practices that take a large portion out of that amount will make a difference, for example, between a parent being able to live at home with children and needing to work, which may significantly enhance the quality of life of a pensioner on a fixed income. The trick to making a garden work for your economic gain is to treat mini-farming as a business. No, it is not a company in terms of registration and taxation because part of its revenue is sold, but it is a company in that, by growing the food spending, it has the same net impact on financing as the profits of a small business. Like any small company, it may make money or lose money based on how it is handled.

Grow Your Own Seedlings Garden centers are filled every spring with home gardeners gathering seedlings for cabbage, broccoli, cucumbers, tomatoes, and so on. To those who grow gardens solely as a hobby, this works well as it helps them to get off to a fast start with limited expenditure in time and preparation. But it's a bad idea for a mini-farmer who practices gardening as a small business.

Such broccoli seed-grown plants saved a lot of money in the long term.

This year, I intend to grow 48 broccoli plants in my own greenhouse. Seedlings from the garden center would have cost $18 if they had been priced and likely over $30. Only the most costly organic broccoli seed on the market cost less than a dollar for 48 seeds. When transplants are grown at home, their effective cost can decrease from $18 to $30 down to $1. Adding to the expense of fertilizer and pots, the expense is only just around $2 for 48 broccoli seedlings. Given that a mini-farm would possibly need transplants for thousands of crops ranging from onion sets to tomatoes and lettuce, it soon becomes evident that even if all seeds are imported, cultivating transplants at home will save hundreds of dollars a year.

Prefer Open-Pollinated Varieties

Two specific forms of seed / plant hybrids are available: hybrid and open-pollinated. Open-pollinated plant varieties produce seeds which replicate the plants that produced them. Hybrid plant varieties produce seeds which are, at best, ineffective and often sterile and thus therefore unusable. While hybrid plants have the downside of not providing good seed, they also have benefits that make it worthwhile, including aspects of 'hybrid vigor.' Hybrid vigor refers to a widely known phenomenon in plants where crossbreeding between two different varieties of broccoli can yield even more robust and successful offspring than either parent.

Based on genetic influences, it also allows the development of plants that combine some of the better characteristics of both parents while de-emphasizing undesirable traits. Through way of hybridization, seed producers are also able to produce varieties of plants that combine disease resistance into a especially strong vegetable crop. Should not only using hybrid seeds? And there's nothing like a free meal. There is no significant change in the vigor of hybrids in plants that are usually self-pollinated, such as peppers and tomatoes. Hybrids are only a proprietary way of marketing. But planting hybrids in those situations actually increases prices, and since tomato seeds can't be spared, the mini-farmer will have to buy seeds again next year. The cost of seed for a family-sized mini-farm that provides much of the family's food for the year will easily be as high as $200, a substantial amount! Beyond that, seed harvested and stored at home can not only minimize prices, but can be resold if properly approved. (Here in New Hampshire, a license to sell seeds costs just $100 a year.) Another justification for saving seeds from open-pollinated plant varieties is that if you save seeds from the best-performing plants every year, you will ultimately produce varieties with genetic characteristics that fit well in your specific soil and environment. That's the sort of training that money can't afford. There are, of course, instances where hybrid seeds and plants outperform the proverbial country mile of open-pollinated varieties. Corn is only one such example. The answer, huh? Using hybrid seeds or, if you're so inclined, make your own!

It's pretty quick to hybridize maize. Hybrid seeds that exhibit specific pest-and disease-resistant characteristics can also be a safe choice when these pests or diseases cause ongoing problems. By growing organic plants, reducing the need for synthetic pesticides is a smart option.

Intensive planting approaches A variety of intensive planting methods have been well documented over the last century. What both of these have in common is growing plants even more widely spaced than conventional rowing methods. This finer separation produces a substantial decrease in the amount of land required to produce a given quantity of food, which in turn greatly decreases requirements for water, fertilizer and mechanization. Since plants are growing close enough together to create a kind of "living mulch," plants shade out weeds and maintain more moisture, minimizing the amount of effort required to produce the same amount of grain.

Intensive planting strategies make a major difference in the amount of room required to have all the food of a individual. Current agrobusiness activities need 30,000 square feet per person or 3/4 acre. Intensive gardening practices that minimize the amount of space needed for the same nutritional content to 700 square feet,6 plus another 700 square feet for crops grown specifically for composting. That's just 1,400 square feet per person, so a family of three can be supplied in just 4,200 square feet.

It's less than 1/10 of an acre. In certain areas of the United States, property is incredibly costly, and the size of the lot is half an acre or less. Using conventional agricultural methods, it is not even feasible to grow food for a single person in a half-acre lot, however by using intensive planting strategies, even half of that lot—1/4 acre — can provide almost all food for a family of four, produce thousands of dollars in revenue, grow small livestock and leave space for home and recreation. Intensive planting methods are the secret to a limited amount of self-sufficiency.

Compost Since growing too many plants in so little space puts a strong pressure on the soil on which they are grown, all intensive farming methodologies pay special attention to preserving soil fertility. The rule on the conservation of matter suggests that, if a farmer grows a plant, the plant has taken nutrients from the soil itself. If the plant is eliminated from the field, the nutrients in the plant will never be added to the soil and soil fertility will be decreased.

Normal agribusiness activities add synthetic fertilizers from outside the field to account for the lack of productivity. The fertilizer, of course, costs money. Although there are other important explanations for limiting the use of non-organic fertilizers, including environmental degradation, the key explanation is that a well-managed soil fertility program will significantly minimize the need to buy fertilizers, thus eliminating one of the major costs associated with farming and making the mini-farm more economically viable.

In practice, a certain amount of fertilizer would still be needed, particularly at the beginning, but using organic fertilizers and composting will effectively reduce the requirements for fertilizer to a bare minimum. The method of maintaining soil fertility consists of growing crops primarily for compost benefit, growing crops to restore ambient nitrogen in the soil, and composting any available crop residues (along with particular compost crops) and almost everything else that is not clogged. (Chapter 5 discusses composting in detail.) A major part of soil productivity is the abundance of microbial life in the soil, as well as the presence of earthworms and other beneficial insects. About 4,000 pounds of bacteria are present in an acre of fertile soil. These species work together with soil nutrients to achieve robust growth and decrease the damage done by disease-causing microorganisms known as "pathogens." Grow Calorie-Dense Crops As already mentioned, vegetables supply just about 10% of average American calories. As a result, a typical vegetable garden will provide outstanding produce and rich vitamin content, but the economic benefit of vegetables does not dramatically reduce your food bill over the course of a year. The solution to this issue is to grow crops that have a higher proportion of caloric needs, such as grapes, dried beans, grains and root crops such as potatoes and onions.

Grow Meat at Home Most Americans are used to having at least a part of their calories from eggs and poultry. Agribusiness meat is often processed using procedures and chemicals (such as growth hormones and antibiotics) that bother a lot of people. Certainly, factory-farmed beef is very high in the least safe fats relative to free-range, grass-fed or hunting-harvested animals. The trouble with meat, in an economic context, is that feeding one calorie of meat usually requires between two and four calories of feed. This looks, at first glance, like a very wasteful use of energy, but it's not as bad as it seems. Most livestock, including small-scale livestock like chickens, get a large portion of their diet from foraging around. Poultry is going to eat all the ticks, fleas, spiders, beetles and grasshoppers that can be found and dispose of the field table scraps. If the meat is grown on the property, so the mini-farmer merely has to collect enough extra food to make up the gap between the feed requirements and what has been collected from scrapping and foraging.

Plant Some fruit A variety of fruits can be grown in most parts of the country: strawberries, grapes, blackberries, pears and cherries, to name a few. Newer dwarf fruit tree varieties frequently grow large quantities of fruit in just three years and take up very little space. Grapes native to North America, such as Concord grapes, are hardy in the western United States, and certain strains, such as muscadine grapes, are abundant in the

South and have recently been shown to provide specific health benefits. Strawberries are easy to produce and appealing to young people. A variety of new varieties of blackberry and raspberry have been introduced, even without thorns, and are so competitive that you'll have more berries than you can think. Fruits are perfect desserts which can be conveniently stored for apple sauce, apple butter, cookies, jellies, pie filling which shortcake topping. Many fruits can also be kept whole for a few months using root cellars. Fruits grown with little to no chemical usage are costly in the supermarket, so growing your own would bring much more money into the bank with limited effort.

Grow Market Crops In particular, if you use organic farming techniques, you can get top-wholesale-dollars for crops sold to supermarkets, organic food cooperatives, and so on. If your property helps, you can even set up a farm stand and market home-grown produce on top of the retail price. A mini-farmer in the United States might hope to receive $2,079 in space income required to feed one human in addition to actually feeding the individual. Assuming a family of three and correcting the USDA recorded an improvement in food value of $10,060 a year during the six-month growing season. Mel Bartholomew's 1985 book Ca$h from Square Foot Gardening reported $5,000 a year in profits over the six-month growing season from a mere 1,500 square feet of well maintained greenhouse. It is equal to $8,064 on today's economy. A mini-farm that sets aside just 2,100 square feet for market crops will have a gross income of $11,289 a year. It is worth noting that two very different agencies have approached very nearly the same estimates for the estimated profit from general selling of vegetables — about $5.00 per square foot.

Season Extension A lot of people don't know that most of Europe, where greenhouses, cold frames, and other seasonal extenders have been used for decades, is north of most of the United States. Maine, for example, is situated at the same latitude as southern France. The explanation for the variation in temperature has to do with ocean winds, not latitude, because latitude is the main influence in deciding the effectiveness of growing protected plants as it determines the amount of sunlight available. In fact, something that can be done in Southern France will be done in the United States of America. The key to making seasonal extension commercially possible lies in collaborating for nature rather than against it. Any effort to create a super-isolated and heated tropical ecosystem ideal for growing bananas in Minnesota in January would be prohibitively costly. A plain, unheated hoop house covered in plastic is relatively inexpensive and will fit extremely well with climate-selected crops.

Extending the season offers two huge benefits. Next, it lets you pick fresh vegetables and seasonal food all year round, including tomatoes, carrots and onions, keeping your family's food costs down. First, it makes for early start-ups and later ends of the main growing season, netting more direct food for the household and more money for the market. It also offers a nice break from harsh winters as a mini-farmer will stroll out to a hop house for fresh salad greens in the midst of a snowstorm.

As a mini-farmer, you can grow food for two markets: the family and the city. The family is the hardest group to consider, since family tastes can be easily found by looking in the refrigerator and cabinets. The society is a harder nut to crack, and if you want to sell your surplus crops, you will need to determine the needs of your society. Food is a commodity, meaning that the vast majority of food is manufactured and sold in gargantuese amounts at low profit margins beyond the control of a mini-farmer. The proportion of crops produced for the market can not be assumed to compete with the purchasing costs of major commercial enterprises.

Therefore, the only way in which a mini-farmer can potentially make a profit is by marketing it directly to the market or through high-markup organics on a wholesale basis. Direct agriculture products will function as well as value-added products such as pickles, salsas and gourmet vinegars. Your goods may appeal to the community in a variety of ways, but the specific solutions that will function in a given case rely on the farmer's interpretation of the needs of the community. You will keep proper notes to ensure that the correct crops are grown.

Economic Calculation According to the Federal Bureau of Labor Statistics, as of October 2005, the average non-farm wage earner in the United States earns $557.54 a week or $28.990 a year for working 40.7 hours a week or 2.116 hours a year. According to the Tax Foundation, the average employee serves 84 out of 260 days a year just to pay taxes withheld from the salary, making the average employee $19,620. According to the 2001 Kenosha County Commuter Report, conducted in Wisconsin before our most recent rise in gasoline prices, the average worker spent $30 a week on petrol only commuting back and forth to work, or $1,500 a year, and spent $45 a week on lunch and coffee going to work, or $2,340 a year. The cost of child care for children under the age of 5 was reported at $297 per month for children under the age of 5 and $224 per month for children between the ages of 5 and 12. This estimation is from the 1997 Urban League report, and there is no question that the cost has risen in the meantime. With a school-age infant, though, the cost of all this adds up enough that the average worker has just $13,092 left over, which can be used to cover the mortgage or rent, the energy bill, and so on.

While there could be other justifications for embracing mini-farming, including quality-of-life problems such as the potential of home-school children, it makes economic sense for one partner in a working family to become a mini-farmer because the net economic benefit of a mini-farm will exceed income from jobs. Obviously, mini-farming would not be a smart economic choice for physicians, attorneys, media moguls, and others with other highly paying professions. Yet mini-farming may have a significant net economic effect that certain jobs can be substituted if the other partner is working in a regular occupation.

Mini-farming is often fairly time-efficient to be able to remove the need for a second work. This may even be done part-time in the evenings as a replacement for tv time. The economy of the mini-farming business looks like this. According to the 2003 Census Bureau estimates, the average household size in the United States is 2.61 individuals. Let's round it up to 3 for quick multiplication. According to figures given earlier, taking into account the rise in food prices, the cost of feeding a family of three is now $3,210 per adult, or $9,630 a year. A mini-farm that produced 85 per cent of those needs would have an average economic gain of $8,185 a year — the same as a pre-tax profit of

$12,200, except that it can not be paid. It will require 2,100 square feet of space, and 10 hours a week from April to September — a total of 240 hours.

It is equivalent to nearly $51 an hour. If the farm also devoted 2,100 square feet to market crops, you will also receive $10,060 over the regular growing season, and devote an extra five hours a week from April to September. That's almost $84 an hour. If cash revenue is added to the economic gain of a sharp decline in grocery costs, the estimated net economic profit of $14,920 beats the total economic gain of actual jobs by about $2,000 a year. It is predicting a lot of worst-case scenarios. It assumes that the mini-farmer does not use any kind of seasonal extension, which would increase the benefit produced, and assumes that the mini-farmer does not subtract all of the payroll expenditures in order to minimize the tax liability. In addition, once automatic irrigation has been installed, the minifarmer will only have to operate three to four hours a day from April to November. Instead of working 2,116 hours a year to net $13,092 after taxes and moving to regular wage earners, the mini-farmer employed just 360 to 440 hours per year to total $14,920. By the close of the working day, the mini-farmer doesn't have to go anywhere — because anywhere is where the farm is, so the workday started early.

In this way, a mini-farmer raises more than 1,500 hours a year that can be used to enhance the quality of life in other ways, enjoys a much healthy diet, performs on a daily basis, and achieves a degree of freedom from the usual structure of jobs. It's difficult to apply a cash figure to it. For families who wish a parent to be at home with a infant who prefer their children at school, mini-farming will make that possible — and raise money in the end by making the adult who makes the least income from a normal job go to mini-farming. It's not a brainer for balanced individuals with a fixed budget.

### Setting up the mini farm

Where do you start when you're a small farmer who never owned a farm before? You can live in the city and want to buy land to start a farm company. And maybe you know it's going to take some time for you to discover your dream farm, but in the meantime, you'd like to do some homesteading in your suburban backyard. This are the ways you can make your little farm dream come true.

When you're always waiting for the right plot of land to turn up, so one thing you can do in the meantime is to know more about farming. Read farm books and magazines on everything related to farming, from how to pick the soil to the best way to raise sheep. See whether you can consider a farm job or an internship and learn the fundamentals of farming firsthand. Immerse yourself in the vocabulary and culture of farming by visiting farms and talking to local farmers who are doing as you would like to do. Know what you can about other producers.

Decide what kind of farm you like, what kind of farm appeals to you? Do you want a small farm company, a hobby farm, or a homestead? Go deep to do a kind of soul searching. If you want to make a living farm, you probably want to start a small farm and look at it as a business. If you're retired or have some money and you want to farm on the side for fun, maybe you want a hobby farm. Homesteaders typically set the target of self-sufficient life, but they often operate small businesses from their homes.

Plan Your Farm

Keep a diary or a code file with notes and suggestions while you learn and speak to people about farming. How the hell strikes your fancy? Do the goats look sexy as a possible farm animal? Do you like the thought of having a diversified farm, where you do a little bit of something, or do you think you want to specialize in one element, maybe an alternate crop or company that's a little off the beaten track?

Allow yourself to have a fantasy. And start planning a small farm.

Project Your Small Farm Business Starting a small farm could mean growing food for your consumption, or even offering extra vegetables and eggs to family and friends. However, you are likely to choose to sell your farm goods, whether on a farmer's market, to supermarkets, to retail retailers or national dealers, to niche food shops or directly to farm customers. There are many options to continue the business aspect of your small farm. Taking one move at a time, such as drafting a business plan, obtaining funding, selling your company, and building a website.

Set up your budget

Determine how much farm you want to purchase. You need to make sure that if you're buying in a poor, very rural place, you're not going to wind up underwater or farm too out of proportion to the area prices that you're going to have a hard time reselling if you need to.

Tailor the quest for what you need and what you can afford. Don't suppose you need hundreds and thousands of acres. Take the time to calculate just how much land you need for your farm goals.

In certain situations, you may not be able to afford to purchase a farm quite yet, so ask that a part-time farm caretaker is right for you. Doing a little farm on the side may just be the hobby you need to wet your whistle.

Get Started

After you've completed all the groundwork, the next step is to get your small farm business started. Have a look at how you can get your company off the ground with some start-up ideas, such as beginning a chicken broiler company, egg business, substitute crops, or pick-your-own farm.

Track and reassess

As you progress through each target of your hobby farm program, you can want to reassess. Be responsive and be flexible about what you learn through the process. Of starters, you might find that raising chickens of meat is more effort than you planned, and that having goats might have to wait a little longer than you anticipated. Ok, be Cool with that. Successful farming is all about being agile and being open to changing the strategy. You should also be faithful to your underlying motives for farming and your grand-picture ambitions.

## Tools and equipments for mini-farming

You know that as a farmer, buying farm tools sounds like a good way to spend a sunny Saturday afternoon. With so many options available and a limited budget, it is difficult to figure out what you need to buy.

View this farm equipment list, which you can use to maintain the farm more efficiently. Hope that some of the following machines will eventually appear on the list of items you want to buy.

1. a tractor

Tractors come in many different sizes, and they are multi-purpose agricultural equipment. Of course, you will choose the right horsepower and the right mounting level for the planned work. Two-wheel tractors-known as walk-behind tractors, can be used with various accessories, including hay bales, rotary tillers, seeders, trucks, orthopedic beds, etc.

2. ATV / UTV

All-terrain vehicles (ATV) and utility vehicles (UTV) are very interesting equipment, and they are also very useful. If you have a large farm, they will save you a lot of time, so you don't have to walk around. You can also use them to haul harvesters or other equipment. They can be used to tow small trailers and provide many attachment options.

3. Agricultural truck

Every farmer should have a truck. Whether you need to travel long distances, pull a trailer or drive through a field, there is a model for you.

4. Truck

Agricultural trucks are the ideal solution for moving hay.

5. Lawn mower

Choose from push-back mowers, horse-riding mowers, zero-turn mowers, belly mowers or push-back mowers to match lawn or pasture maintenance. If you want hay, you may need a sickle mower, drum mower or disc mower. For large areas, consider using lawn mowers, bat mowers and even fl mowers to collect your agricultural equipment.

6. Backhoe

If you need tools for digging holes, please buy a backhoe. The backhoe can be used as a separate hydraulic implement for different types of tractors.

7. Plastic coating

If your farm uses a plastic cultivation method, it must be equipped with a plastic cover attachment for the tractor.

8. Sprayer

The sprayer is used to apply compost tea, herbicides and pesticides.

## 9. Irrigation system

Without continuous water supply, your crops will not grow well. You can choose an irrigation system, such as a highly permeable hose, or a complex multi-stage drip irrigation system to water the crops.

## 10. Sickle

The sickle is one of the oldest agricultural tools and is still useful for small farmers. Although it is not as effective as a lawnmower, it can still be used to trim tall grass and shrubs.

## 11. Sickle

The sickle is a hand-held cutting tool used for harvesting or mowing grass, and can be used for small applications.

## 12. Rake

If you want to make hay and there are several different types, rakes are essential, including wheel rakes, parallel bar rakes, rotation rate and belt rakes.

## 13. Baler

There are three types of hay baler: square baler, round baler and large square baler.

14. Combine harvester

Grain farmers absolutely need to have a combine harvester in order to harvest crops, because they are the most effective tool for removing crops from the field.

15. Manure spreader

Manure spreaders are very useful in horse farms. However, you should also ensure that you read about fertilizer spreading techniques to avoid the spread or contamination of parasites caused by fecal runoff.

16. Hydroponics

Hydroponics is a system for growing plants in water instead of using soil. Compared to a soil-cultivated garden, this will allow you to use less water to grow large amounts of food. You can also grow crops indoors.

17. Seeding machine

The planter is an attachment to the tractor and is used to insert seeds into the ground while minimizing disturbance to the soil. No-till drip irrigation is designed to remove existing crop residues, thereby creating a path for planting new seeds.

18. Front-end loader

Front-end loaders can be used to connect to trackers to dig, move large items and lift heavy objects.

## 19. Ploughing machine

Tillage machines are used for soil cultivation to prepare seed beds or control weeds before planting onto the beds.

## 20. Cultipacker

The tiller packer is designed to be pulled by a tractor to reinforce the seedbed before sowing so that the seeds can maintain good contact with the soil during sowing.

## 21. Plow

There are many types of plows, you may need a combination of several plow heads to meet your farming needs. Choose from a scraper plow, chisel plow and disc plow depending on the type of crop to be planted, soil type and land condition.

## 22. Rake

The harrow is designed to be pulled behind the tractor or ATV to level the soil surface.

## 23. Broadcast Seeder

The planter has various shapes and is designed to distribute seeds in a specific area. You can use them to grow crops, forage and grass.

## 24. Transplanting machine

The transplanter has tractor-tractable and hand-held options to meet your farming requirements. There are many models, they can use the foot motion or hand motion to activate the lever in the transplanter, so that the plant can fall directly into the hole dug by the tool.

## How to take care of your mini-farm

You may have thought about starting your own mini-farm, but you do not know where to go. Some people would like to work with Australian backpackers because they like the thought of living on a farm. Some people want to offer backpackers jobs in the town, and you can do that by starting a mini-farm. Keep reading to learn how to set up a mini-farm that will become your pride and joy.

1. Find A Good Land Plot: Your land plot doesn't need to be very that, but you need enough space to develop the stuff you want to develop. Many people will find land in an allotment, while many will start a mini-farm on their own lands. If you've found a good place, you can start planting right away. Plus, at any given time, you can monitor how many crops are on the farm.

2. Import Top Soil And Fertilizer: You need to import topsoil and fertilizer and be sure that it is growing the way it should be. If you use the correct topsoil and fertilizer, you'll get even better results. Plus, you need to start by checking one or two plants to

see how much topsoil and fertilizer you need. You will top up your grin a year before planting again.

3. Organise the farm: You need to organise the farm in such a manner that you have room for all the things you want to plant. Many plants can be cultivated in very small spaces, but other crops require a lot of space to grow. After you've arranged it all, you can plant like a professional farmer.

4. Plant Products You Think You Can Sell: You Should Plant Crops You Think You Can Sell. When you can not sell crops on your farm, you need to learn how to do them yourself. Most of the people who start a mini-farm are looking to make a little profit, and that's why you need to be sure you've known what the market for your crops is going to be.

5. Climate and Flood : You need to monitor rainfall and flooding in the region as best you can. You should dig French trenches around your plot to bring water down to the lower level of the house. You could dig a wide trench around the plot to help drain water, and you could water your crops on a timetable so they won't get waterlogged. It is a big part of caring for your seeds, as you don't want them to die until they're fully grown.

6. Using Organic Pesticides: The mini-farm does not have a license to use pesticides that are found in big crops. Because of this, it makes a lot of sense for you to use natural ingredients that do not cause any harmful effects in the environment. A lot

of consumers will choose to buy the natural goods they produce at home, and there are some who will add their own insect bugs to the surplus. You can handle pests on your own if you've done your homework.

7. Be patient: You need to be careful when growing crops in your mini-farm. The mini-farm is a spot where you'll have to wait for all the plants to grow to full size. You should create a list of dates and times that you can conveniently keep track of while you're planting, and you should adhere to the calendar as best as you can. When the schedule is complete, you will use the same schedule any time you plant it.

# Chapter Three
## Raising Beds

Mini-farming is feasible due to elevated beds and correctly formed soil. Young people in the developed world have a lot less free time and a lot less ground than their ancestors did. Raised beds deliver so many benefits over row gardens that it's hard to imagine why everyone but major agribusiness companies doesn't use them. For northern climates for particular, raised beds can help gardeners extend their growing season as they can increase surface temperatures by 8 to 13 degrees relative to surface temperatures. Through raising the soil level, growers and gardeners will start their crops early so the excess moisture disappears quickly enough that the cold spring rains will not kill new crops.

The elevated beds could often conveniently compatible with fittings, such as cold frames. A raised bed is basically a bottomless, topless box laid on the ground and lined with dirt. The boxes may be made of timber, plastic sheets, cement and other materials. Raised beds may be constructed from terracotta, but covering them with a box construction prevents the deterioration of the carefully planned soil of the area. Raised beds prolong the season and increased the issues associated with hot rainfall.

Product Choices The foundations of the elevated beds are in direct contact with wet soil and could be rotting. Ordinary lumber can last two or three years before replacement is needed. This can be avoided by properly coating the exposed surfaces of the frames with a water-based outer latex paint and allowing them to dry completely before using it. Should not use oil-based paints or paints with anti-moulding additives, or else you will poison the dirt in your rooms. Due to the weight of the dirt, the boards used should be at least 1.5 inches thick to prevent bowing, and the opposite sides of long runs should be bound together every eight feet or so.

The biggest advantages of timber are its quick supply and ease of service. Ordinary concrete blocks are inexpensive and easy to use. These are easily available, durable, and strong enough to support the soil in a raised bed without mortar. These can be picked up and moved around to move or change tents, which can be reused nearly forever. The biggest drawback is their weight—45 pounds on both of them. This means that, given their small dimensions, only 22 can be transported at a time in a pick-up truck estimated to haul half a ton.

Since each block is 18 inches wide, the pick-up load is just 33 linear feet long. Boards made of recycled plastic used for decks and other outdoor construction have become more readily available in recent years and combine the simple handling of conventional lumber with the toughness of concrete blocks. There are some raised-bed kits on the market that use plastic sheets, and they may be a good choice if you're intending to do a small amount of gardening, but because of the size of the kits, they don't make sense on the scale needed to feed the family.

Cut money for a mini-farm by purchasing wooden boards from the lumber store and chopping them to the right size yourself. It is possible that more modern pressure-treated lumber uses fewer toxic materials than it used to, but the materials are still harmful and can leach into the soil of the developing bed so that they are better avoided.

Built beds may be constructed of a range of materials. This one is made of cinder blocks and landscape trees. Several different materials may be used, from landscaping to poured concrete types. Only let the ingenuity, cost, longevity, and possible toxicity of something you might use drive your decision. Bear in mind when using materials when leach pesticides in growing beds totally undermines the intent of the home garden or mini-farm because eating items grown in such beds can be highly dangerous. (Arsenic in pressure treated wood, for example, is both directly poisonous and potentially carcinogenic.) Shape and design of raised beds The most typical and most useful type for raised beds is rectangular.

Most flower planters are oval, and this fits well as long as the width is not so wide that the gardener needs to walk into the field. Another each form is a square of 4 feet. This works well for casual vegetable gardening-only on a small scale, but on the scale of supplying all the family's needs, it is a waste of room and resources. I prefer a rectangular shape as it allows full use of space and limited material while making it easier to install uniform structures such as hoop houses. Every rectangular bed is going to be longer than the big one. To provide full sunlight to crops and prevent shade, ensure that the long sides face north and south. Any trellising for vine-growing crops should be built along the northern edge in order to benefit from sunlight without shading other crops.

Height of raised beds: Distance Everybody has an view about the height of raised beds. The Grow Biointensive approach prefers a width of 5 feet and a length of 20 feet to create a "microclimate" for intensive agriculture. Square Foot fans recommend a fixed width of 4 feet, as it is easy to enter a bed that is 4 feet long on either side and to get to whatever is in the centre. Many successful organic growers are using only narrower raised beds. The five-foot diameter proposed by Ecology Action allows multiple individuals to walk onto the bed on a board built to distribute the weight more evenly and reduce disruption to the soil structure. But reaching the garden bed at all, including using a surface, undermines the objective of careful maintenance of the soil structure by compacting the dirt.

The board will have to be set up so that it could be spread over the sides of the bed frame and be sturdy enough not to bend while anyone is standing on it. (This would not be feasible with the full Grow Biointensive approach because, in that system, the raised beds are just mounded soil without structural sides. My method uses structural sides instead.) The 4-foot width is small enough that most people can access the garden from both sides since only a 2-foot access is required. However, this does not work as trellised crops growing food on both sides of the trellis expand against one of the long sides of the shelter. In this case, for example, harvesting pole beans requires a 4-foot radius, which most people don't have.

Height of elevated beds: length We do know that beds have to be rectangular for economic purposes and three to four feet deep for convenience — but how long will they be? Technically, they can be as long as the farmer needs, but there are several elements of duration worth considering. One of the major causes of insect and disease problems is growing the same plants in the same field year after year. Bacterial, fungal, and viral diseases sometimes favor host plants — and often do not even emerge in unrelated plants.

Although these pathogens interact with more beneficial microbes in compost-rich soil, they can only live for a short amount of time — usually three years or less — in soil that does not have an adequate host. Insect pests (some of which transmit diseases) are somewhat similar. They have a particular appetite

— a particular niche — for eg, cabbage. Not only can these pests consume cabbage and inject it with diseases, but they also lay their eggs in the soil around the cabbage so that their offspring can emerge right next to their favorite meal. One effective way to thwart these predators is to make sure that they choose plants that are not appetizing as their offspring wake up in the morning.

Limiting the length of the raised beds so that you have enough space to build a couple of them makes it easier to perform crop rotation as the soil in one bed is separated from the soil in the other. Making sure that the same crop is not cultivated in the same bed for three years solves a lot of issues in advance. In my own mini-farm, beds are 8 to 24 feet tall.

Start at the Right Time and Grow Slowly

The time between when the soil can be first worked in the spring and when early spring crops are to be planted is around three weeks. It's just not enough time to build adequate raised beds. At the end of the day, you would need around 700 square feet per person for complete food self-sufficiency. If you're trying to grow market crops, you're going to need more. That's going to take a lot of rooms. The number will depend on the amount of time you pick. Assuming that beds are 4-feet × 25-feet, that means that you need at least seven beds per person or 21 beds for a family of three. Using 4-feet × 8-feet beds will be 22 beds per person or 66 for a family of three.

For reality, based on nutritional requirements, chosen crop types, climate and other considerations, a greater or smaller number of beds may potentially be required. The initial construction of raised beds requires a substantial amount of time and is very labour-intensive, but once they have been built, relatively little effort is required to sustain them. Raised beds can be generated in a variety of ways, but even the most time-efficient solutions can require a couple of hours per bed. When you have little time, it would be practically difficult to have all the beds made in the morning. Therefore, the best time to start mini-farming is the summer or the fall before the first growing season.

This way the beds can be prepared in a more leisurely way and then sown with cover crops for overwintering. You just have to cut the cover crops in the spring, place them in the compost pile, maintain established gardens, and continue planting. It could be better to start mini-farming slowly — say, by first making enough beds for a single individual's food — and then keep adding beds as time and resources allow until the appropriate amount has been created. It's because of a trade-off between time and money. If the prospective farmer has the time to set up all the beds he wants originally, that's fine. But if time is limited, the only way to shorten the scheme is to pay for heavy equipment and compost truck loads.

I don't want the fact that fall is the perfect time to get going to deter you from starting either in the spring or in the summer, if that's when you want to start. It's always easier to start than to wait, since only a few raised beds will yield a lot of food. If you get moving in the spring or the summer, just bear in mind that you're going to install fresh beds in the fall.

Creating beds For purposes of economy and efficiency, I suggest the construction of beds initially by double digging. Lay out the area to be mined using the stakes and the string, and, once drilled, cover the area with the material you have selected to build the bed frame. As the simultaneous digging method would remove the dirt, the depth of the dug area will be between four and six inches higher than the surrounding soil. Double digging has been a traditional agricultural method for soil enhancement in different parts of the world for untold centuries, and that is what I recommend because it is the most productive for the resources required.

The theory behind double digging is that plants take their roots deep into the earth, and ensuring that there are nutrients and aerated earth two feet deep offers perfect growth conditions. However, the asparagus grown in a double bed was much superior to any other. While certain plants, particularly grasses, can send roots a few feet deep, the majority of the root system of the plant is located in the top six inches of the soil. This implies, of course, that double digging is not the only acceptable way to prepare the soil for mini-farming. Apparently, there are three methods to dig beds.

Digging Techniques The old-timers I grew up in never used the word dual digging. In the United States and the United Kingdom, this method has traditionally been known as "bastard trenching" to differentiate it from "real" or "absolute" trenching. Most modern texts don't mention it, but there are really three kinds of trenches that are useful in various circumstances. These three types of trenching are incredibly hard work, especially in areas with a lot of large rocks or soils consisting mostly of clay, but they provide value-for-money benefits. Such three types of trenches are pure drilling, bastard trenching, and trenching. Plain digging depends on the use of a garden spade to dig in and bring the dirt to the size of a single spade.

The field to be dug shall be marked out by means of a line or other marking, and the garden spade shall be used to dig the land one-spread wide and one-spread deep across the width of the plot, and the soil shall be put in a wheelbarrow. So a few layers of compost is applied to the bottom of the first trench, and the soil from the next adjacent trench is transferred to the surface of the compost in the first trench. This process continues until the last trench is dug and manure applied to the ground, and the soil collected from the first trench is transferred to the hole created by the last trench. The only difference between simple digging and double digging (a.k.a. son of a bitch trenching) is that in the latter, after the trench is digged a single digging deep and before the compost is inserted, a digging fork is placed into the soil at the bottom of the trench to raise and break up the dirt. Finally, more compost is applied to the surface and combined with the remaining six inches of dirt.

Both simple digging and double digging can be helpful for freshly formed fields and can be extremely useful for areas filled with grass because soil spits (the soil that makes up the spade-full is known because "spit") can be pushed down in the adjacent trench when they are dug. In this case, where weeds or grass has traditionally been used for planting, it is highly beneficial to sift through the soil and extract wireworms and grubs as you go along. When I use one of these trenching techniques, not only do I place compost in the bottom of the trenches, but I apply some to the top of the finished bed and mix it in as well. Garden fork and digging spade are important tools for simultaneous digging.

True or full trenching is a dangerous challenge, but it is necessary to restore soil in fields that have already been duplicated or where the soil can be worked extensively without the use of a backhoe. A well-maintained bed would never have to be regenerated, but real trenching can be helpful when working with land that was historically overgrown using traditional techniques, as the subsoil is replaced with the top soil. In the actual trench, the first trench is dug a single-spread deep and the soil is dug from that set aside, and then the same trench is dug another spade down, and the soil is set aside as well, apart from the soil from the top of the trench. Then a digging fork is used to break up the dirt in the bottom as far as the tines, and compost is applied. When the second adjacent trench is dug, the spits from the top are attached to the bottom of the first trench, and the spits from the bottom are applied to the top of the trench.

The topsoil is covered in this manner, and the subsoil is taken to the top. Start this way until the last trench is filled, where the top spits of the first trench are put in the bottom of the last trench, and then those spits are covered with the remaining ones. Since true trenching transfers the topsoil to the subsoil, and subsoil appears to contain even less organic matter, ample quantities of aged compost should be applied to the top sheet, treated properly, and left to settle for a few weeks until the new bed can be used. In each of the three trenching techniques, you can use hand tools to push, practically, thousands of pounds of soil for each bed. This can be grueling work, so you can only use spades so digging forks that have been bought or adjusted to match your height.

The right height of a spade or fork (plus handle) can be measured by standing the implement directly next to you, then seeing how far it hits your neck. The tip of the handle is meant to be somewhere between your forearm and the center of your breastbone. Digging forks and spades can be bought with either a straight or a "D" stick. You will get the "D" models, because they will reduce the amount of back twisting needed. Hold the back straight while using the device, so stop any spinning so pussy motions. Function at a relaxed pace, and take a break when needed. This offers you an outstanding and healthy aerobic exercise that increases your strength and endurance while improving the soil.

What's about "No-Dig" beds?

In my experience, I have seen little that competes, in terms of sheer efficiency, with dual beds raised properly. However, that may be a lot of work, and people with no energy or physical disabilities do not want to make the effort. You can still get really good results, though, using a non-dig process.

- Boards are used to mark the new bed. You may use string or chalk almost as easily.
- The first row was drilled.
- Loosing the dirt.
- Add compost to it.
- The digging of the second trench. Beware of the author's trendy feet!
- Putting the spits upside down in the trench.

Functional compost in the top few inches of the new garden. Work any extra compost in the top few inches of the finished bed. As you can see from the photo demonstration, preparing raised beds by double digging is a fairly simple and very physical process. It's a perfect workout that loosens the surface to a depth of two feet, bringing the plant material all the way there. The yields from the beds I work like this are amazing!

Save the old newspapers — only the black-and-white bits, not the shiny bits. In the fall, build a frame of 2×4 lumber right on the field. Lay down several layers of thick sheets, and then cover the bed full with completed compost. Don't miss the newspapers if they're supposed to smother the grass below. If the grass isn't smothered, even if you're just using 2×4 lumbar, you'll end up with a lot of grass growing in the field. As spring comes around and the field thaws, just use the digging fork to fluff it up a little; then plant it, and you're done.

In the case of no-dig beds, it is especially important to keep them planted with cover crops during the off-season because you rely on the activity of the roots of the plant to mix the soil and hold it loose. Since seeds do not always germinate well in compost, I would consider using a bed for transplanted crops for the first year, and then a decent soil creator like beans for the second year. You should view this in all other respects much as a standard elevated bed. If fresh compost is applied regularly, the efficiency would be the same after three years as for a double bed.

Trellising for Raised Beds: Robust Trellising Device Trellising is required for some crops and can be a beneficial complement to certain crops. Since raised beds do not have much room for spreading plants such as cucumbers or poppy beans, the addition of trellis makes growing these crops more realistic and space-efficient. Many crops are more competitive in vineyard versions than in bush versions. These include beans, peas, cucumbers, tomatoes, and more. Pole beans, for example, can yield almost twice as much output per square foot as bush beans. This means that a row of pole beans grown on a trellis on the north side of an 8-foot bed with just 8 square feet of space will yield nearly as many beans as 16 square feet of bush beans. The same estimate extends to other vegetables.

Electrical conduit makes a strong and flexible trellis.

As described earlier in the book, beds are preferably placed with long sides facing north and south. Trellises is to be built on the north side. If, for whatever reason, this alignment is not possible, the second best choice is to have a long side on which the trellises would be placed on the northwest or, in the worst case, on the west side. Do not lay the trellises on the south or east side of the house, or they will cover the sunniest crops during the daytime.

There are as many means of erecting trellises as there are growers, and over the years I have used several different techniques. Over the last two years, my favorite trellising approach has been the use of rebars, electrical conduits, and pipe fittings. The electrical cable is 10 feet tall. Through cutting it to suitable lengths and using correct fittings, it may differ in height and weight. Through placing it over the rebar pushed into the wall, you can quickly pick it off the rebar in the fall for transport, and shifting it to another bed is a breeze. As the timber used to build the beds is eight feet tall, the longest pipe you need is eight feet long. That is for the horizontal section at the end. In the meanwhile, trellis heights will range from two legs for peas to four legs for tomatoes to six legs for pole beans.

A trellis height of more than six feet is not a smart idea, because hitting the top will be tiring or — even worse if a stool is needed — dangerous. The easiest way to get a compact framework is to buy a 10-foot pipe length of six sections at a time. Three are cut into an 8-foot and a 2-foot section, two are cut into a 6-foot and a 4-foot section, and the final length of the pipe is divided into two 4-foot pieces and one 2-foot pieces. When finished, there are three 8-foot horizontals, two 6-foot verticals, four 4-foot verticals, and four 2-foot verticals. In addition to these, you'll need six 90-degree elbows, four screw couplings, and six 2-foot rebar bits for every six sections of pipe. (You can find the rebar already cut to length and packaged at Home Depot and similar stores.) After the rebar is hammered into the ground on either end of the frames, you can fully install or disassemble a trellis of any height from 2-foot to 8-foot in two-foot intervals using a screwdriver.

Total Trellis Formation, Step by Step 1. Hammer 2-foot bits of rebar into the earth at each end of the raised bed, leaving 6 inches off the ground.

Moving the rebar to the bottom.

Placing an upright position over the rebar. Attach the lateral to the curve.

The deck screws were bored to the bottom and protruding 3/8 inch.

1. Race the string between the horizontal screws and the deck screws.

2. Slip the vertical portion of the pipe over the rebar. Repeat for the other hand.

3. Connect the 90-degree elbow to each vertical piece of duct, then connect the horizontal duct to the elbows.

4. Place the deck screws on the side of the raised bed around the trellis every 6 to 12 inches. Left them for only a fifth of an inch.

5. Drag the rope between the horizontal bar on the roof and the deck screws on the side of the raised bed.

6. You've got a full trellis now!

# Chapter Four

## Soil composition and maintenance

The productivity and fertility of the farm and the pest and disease tolerance of the plant depend on the quality of the soil. The soil quality can be improved and the outside nutrients minimized by adequate tillage, compost, field cover and crop rotation. These are crucial to preserving the high degree of fertility needed for near plant spacing in a mini-farm without wasting a lot of money on fertilizers. When French Intensive Gardening was established, horses were the normal mode of transport, and horse manure was abundant and basically free. This describes the reliance on horse manure as a source of soil fertility.

According to the Colorado State University Cooperative Extension Service, the typical 1,000-pound horse produces 9 tons—18,000 pounds — of manure consuming about 730 cubic feet each year. 7 The sheer scale, the scent, and the mess of such a amount of manure always mean that the places on board horses would give it up for asking someone willing to take it up.

Horse manure should be composted and not immediately applied to the bed. Horse manure is also suitable fodder for crops. Pursuant to the same source, horse manure contains 19 pounds of nitrogen per load, 14 pounds of phosphate and 36 pounds of potassium. It amounts to around 1% nitrogen, 0.7%

phosphate and 1.8% potassium. There is no such thing as a free meal, and horse manure is no different. Raw horse manure can spread a parasitic protozoan called giardia and E.coli as well as contaminate water supplies and streams with coliform bacteria. Raw manure can also include worm eggs that are easily spread to humans, including pinworms and various types of ascarid worms. Horse manure is rich in salts and, if used unnecessarily, can cause the plants grown in it to experience water stress, even if well watered.

The average allowable amount of application of horse manure, assuming the least detectable salinity, is between two and three pounds of manure per square foot a year.8 In addition to the objections set forth above, horse manure does not have a sufficient phosphorus element, which ensures that it should be supported by a phosphorus supply as using. Clear horse manure is also in the composting method. That is, the cycle has not yet been completed. Unfinished compost also contains phytotoxic substances that impede the growth of plants. To order for horse manure to be properly available as a planting tool, it must first be well rotted, meaning that either it should be composted in a pile combined with other compost ingredients, such as plant litter, or at least it should be rotted for at least one year before use. The former process is preferred as it can maintain some of the essential nitrogen content of the manure. Potential issues posed by horse manure are avoided by first composting the manure with other materials and then liberally adding the resulting compost to the beds.

The composting cycle should destroy any bacteria, dilute the salinity and remove phytotoxins. Creating the right soil from scratch, on a small scale, works pretty well. The Square Foot Gardening Process uses a mixture of 1/3 coarse vermiculite, 1/3 peat moss, and 1/3 composting by volume and a combination of organic fertilizers to create a "good soil mix." 9 My own experience on a 120-square-foot raised bed shows that the approach works perfectly. The quality of the components is appropriate for small beds.

Only four cubic feet of each part will be needed for a six-inch-deep 4-foot × 6-foot bed. Gross vermiculite and peat moss are now available for around $18 for a four-foot sphere. Assuming free fertilizer, the cost of producing a good soil mix is $1.50 per square foot of growing area. This works very well on a small scale, but when only 700 square feet of land are placed into agricultural cultivation, the expense may become prohibitive.

Double-digging has been discussed in the previous chapter, and this is what I propose for mini-farming. While it is more challenging at first, it offers the best chance to cultivate the best available soil for the resources spent. No-dig beds, which are also mentioned in the previous chapter, are a second choice.

Water-Holding Power and pH No soils are suitable for intensive cultivation or some type of cultivation. Others are so dry, others too rich in clay. Some are too acidic, others too alkaline. Most lack one or two main nutrients and trace minerals. Soil for agricultural use has to retain water without being waterlogged. Sandy soils are rarely waterlogged, but they dry up so easily that continuous watering is required. They make root growth quick, but do not hold on to nutrients very well and are poor in organic or humus material. (There is some disagreement between scholars as to the exact concept of humus. For our purposes, it can be characterized as organic matter in the soil that has reached the point of being so solid that it can not readily be further decomposed. Therefore, finished compost and humus are similar for our purposes.) Clay soils can be waterlogged in the winter and will remain waterlogged as long as water reaches the point of decomposition. So long as the water ends, they're boiling and splitting, squeezing the root systems. Clay soil is clingy, brittle, and almost impenetrable to trees. Loam soil is similar to the ideal, because it consists of a combination of sand and clay with a large quantity of humus, which helps to preserve water and nutrients in quantities appropriate for cultivation. Sandy and clay soils can be enhanced with vermiculite. Vermiculite is created by heating the mica rock in the oven until it looks like popcorn. The effect is a robust material that retains and releases water like a sponge and increases the water-holding properties of almost any kind of soil. If it's an insoluble stone, it's going to survive for decades and even longer. Unless the soil in your bed is not loamy to begin with, adding coarse to medium vermiculite at a rate of 4 to 8 cubic feet per 100 square feet of raised bed would be very useful. (Vermiculite costs $4 per cubic foot in four cubic foot bags at the time of writing.) If you can't find vermiculite, look for peat moss balls instead. Peat moss is an organic substance created from dried ancient vegetation at the bottom of the bogs that swamps and has the same properties as vermiculite in terms of serving as a water source. It costs almost the same and can also be packed in wide balls. It can be applied at the same rate as vermiculite — from four to eight cubic feet per 100 square feet of raised bed. Bear in mind that peat moss reduces the pH of the soil marginally over time and is decomposed, meaning that it has to be recycled.

Vermiculite increases the soil's water retaining ability.

The term pH applies to whether the soil becomes acidic or alkaline and is defined on a scale from 0 to 14, with 0 referring to strongly acidic battery acid, 14 to extremely alkaline drain cleaner and 7 to neutral distilled water. As you might expect, most plants grown in the garden should do well with a pH of between 6 and 7. (There are a few examples, such as blueberries, which require a strongly acidic soil.) pH influences other factors indirectly, including how nutrients still in the soil are suitable for use by plants and the existence of other plant disease species such as 'club foot' in cabbage. In the basis of a pH check, the soil will be modified to either neutral or mildly acidic, pH 6.5 or so, with commercially available lime and sulphur products.

To change the pH up to 1 level, add dolomitic limestone at a rate of 5 pounds per 100 square feet of raised bed and work into the top two inches of soil. To change the pH down to 1 level, apply iron sulfate at a rate of 1.5 pounds per 100 square feet of raised bed and work into the soil. To change the pH by half a level, say from 6 to 6.5, cut the volume by one hundred square feet in half. Changes to pH don't work easily. Wait 40 to 60 days after the additives have been applied, and then re-test the soil before applying any more. If they are applied too fast, they can build up in the soil and make it inhospitable for growing stuff.

Fertilizers The soil fertility is determined by its nitrogen, phosphorus and potassium content, and fertilizers are graded the same using a sequence of numbers called "NPK." N in NPK stands for nitrogen, P for phosphate, and K for potassium. The fertiliser bag will be branded with the NPK in a format that lists the percentage value of each resource, separated by dashes. And, for example, the "5-10-5" fertilizer bag is 5% nitrogen, 10%

phosphate and 5% potassium. A fully degraded garden soil with no measurable NPK amounts needs just 4.6 ounces of N, 5 ounces of P and 5.4 ounces of K per 100 square feet to create a "good" soil. In the case of root crops, less than 3 ounces of N is required. Inexpensive soil samples are available to check soil pH, nitrogen, phosphorus and potassium content. A few weeks after the soil in the bed has been prepared and compost and/or manure has been put in, you can check the nutrient content of the soil and change it accordingly. The most crucial element in your soil's long-term stability is organic matter produced by compost and manure, so just make sure that there is plenty of organic matter first, and then check and see what kind of fertilization is required.

For most garden centers, you can purchase a soil check kit, and most of them offer results for each nutrient as being depleted, insufficient, adequate or necessary. The latter two examples can be misleading, as they have the same meaning as ordinary English. For the purpose of evaluating soil samples, assume "adequate" to mean that enough of the measured nutrient is sufficient for plants to survive but not necessarily to flourish. If the soil check shows the sum to be "sufficient," then there is enough nutrient to sustain optimum production.

When planning a garden, I suggest adding enough organic fertilizers to make all three main nutrients "appropriate." Organic fertilizers are a better option than synthetic fertilizers for a variety of reasons. Plant fertilizers break down more efficiently so that they live longer in the soil and help build up the organic content of the soil when it breaks down. Synthetics will definitely get the job done in the short term, but they do have the ability to damage essential soil microbial diversity that helps deter plant diseases, as well as to damage soil worms and other beneficial soil occupants. For these purposes, I firmly condemn the use of synthetic fertilizers. Organic fertilizers, such as organic fertilizers, are graded NPK, but since they are produced from plant, animal and mineral compounds, they include a broad variety of trace minerals that plants often require. The flavor is perhaps the strongest reason in terms of using organic fertilizers. Hydroponic hothouse tomatoes in the grocery store are grown using only organic mixtures of soil. Compare the taste of hydroponic tomatoes with the taste of organic tomatoes in the garden, and the result should be simple. There is one thing to bear in mind about organic fertilizers: all of them are very appetizing to rodents! One morning, I found that the fertilizer in my garage had been ripped open by red squirrels and had been eaten almost entirely! Since then, I have been holding organic fertilizers in five-gallon buckets with lids.

There are a variety of options available for organic fertilizers. Some of them come premixed, or you may create them from individual components yourself. It's easy to make your own premixed fertilizer. You may use alfalfa meal, soya meal, or blood meal for N. Bone meal and rock phosphate work well for P. Wood ashes, green grass, and seaweed will work for K. The above collection is far from comprehensive, but the products are readily available from most garden or farm shops.

There is still no need to produce an unused soil fertilizer because it is not supposed to happen in the first year, and maybe not even if sufficient compost has been applied. If this is the case, just add triple or quadruple the quantity required for sufficient soil. It should be very quick to produce a few ready-made fertilizers. A "high nitrogen" fertilizer for vegetative crops such as spinach may consist of a mixture of 10 ounces of blood meal, 6 ounces of bone meal and 21 ounces of wood ashes. As long as you keep the proportions the same, you can add as much of it as you want, and you know that 37 ounces of the mixture is needed for every 100 square feet. Only a bit over two pounds.

A low nitrogen fertilizer for root crops such as parsnips may consist of a mixture of 34 ounces of alfalfa meal, 4 ounces of rock phosphate and 30 ounces of green sand. Just as in the first version, as long as you keep the proportions the same, you can add as much as you want, so you know that 68 ounces are needed for every 100 square feet — a hair of more than 4 pounds. Your particular preference of fertilizers and blends will rely on the quality and price of the ingredients, so using a combination of products means that at some stage nearly every known nutrient — and every unknown nutrient — finds its way into your garden beds. Wood ashes can not be used more frequently than once per three years because of the salts they will bring into the soil also because they may raise the pH of the soil.

Fertilizers can be applied to the soil a few weeks before planting and used in the garden bed; any extra fertilizer can then be introduced to the soil as a side covering, probably mixed 50/50 with some dried manure. The explanation for dilution is that certain organic fertilizers, such as blood meal, are very powerful — as effective as synthetic — and, if they directly affect crop foliage, they will kill plants. Liquid fertilizers are worth noting, in particular those meant to be added directly to the leaves. They seem to be highly dilute and they won't harm the plants, so they're a decent option to alleviate transplant pain. For some situations, liquid fertilizers can be life-saving.

Popular organic liquid fertilisers. As an experiment, I applied a thick side-dressing of mixed blood meal, bone meal, and wood ashes to all the cabbage plants, except for half of them, I also watered the leaves with a watering can containing liquid fertilizer combined according to product instructions. In a result, all the plants watered with liquid fertilizer survived and ultimately thrived, although a full half of the plants that provided only side-dressing died.

Soil Conservation

Whether you believe it or not, soil is a fragile material. It's more than just fragile, it's actually alive. It is the vitality of the earth, not its sand and clay, which makes it fertile and productive. A single tablespoon of healthy garden soil contains millions of bacteria, nearly every one of which makes a beneficial contribution to the garden. Organic matter acts as a pH barrier, detoxifies contaminants, retains moisture and preserves nutrients in a fixed state to prevent them from escaping out of the soil.

Some bacteria, such as actinomycetes, send out fragile microscopic chains that extend for miles, giving the soil its structure. The soil structure for intensive agriculture is preserved by cover crops (explained later in this chapter) to preserve fertility and avoid erosion; periodically incorporate organic matter in the form of left over roots, compost and manure; crop rotation; and protect soil from erosion, compaction and loosening. If the soil in the bed has been initially prepared, as long as it has not been compacted, there will be no need for more than a fluffing with a big fork or digging fork every year and stirring up the top few inches with a three-tone cultivator.

The drilling after the creation of the bed is much smoother and quicker than the original double drilling. An occasional eventual footprint does not destroy life on earth, but an attempt can be made to prevent it, as that footprint compacts the soil, making the soil region less likely to retain water, lowers the oxygen that can be retained in the soil in that region, and destroys the structure of the soil, including the stability of old roots and fragile microbial webs. Almost all forms of actinomycets are aerobic — meaning they require oxygen. Compacting the soil could deprive them of the oxygen they need.

Microbial webs in the soil are particularly important because they function in symbiosis with root systems to enhance their spread and ability to assimilate nutrients.10 Damage to these microbial webs — which can extend from the plant for several feet in each direction — reduces the plant's ability to obtain nutrients from the soil. The lesson is clear: optimum production from a raised bed requires preventing soil compression. Some gardeners favor heavy-duty tilling of agricultural land at least annually and sometimes at the beginning and end of the season.

The problem with these practices is that the same facets of soil life and structure that are disturbed by compaction are also disturbed by tilling, especially deep tilling. Modifications of soil, such as compost and organic fertilizers, will be combined with soil — no way. But this does not require a rototiller. A plain, hand-operated, three-toned cultivator (like a claw) is necessary to integrate amendments into the top few inches of soil. Earthworms and other soil occupants must work to disperse compost to dense soil layers.

The Incredible Power of Biochar: Many of us are used to speaking of charcoal as an important resource for grilling, and it definitely is! Less well known, however, is its similarly beneficial effect when applied to ordinary garden soil. The regular carbon that you purchase in the grocery store may be impregnated with anything from saltpeter to volatile organic compounds meant to make you combust, and it may not be a safe option. There are some "natural" or even organic charcoals out there that can be used, such as Cowboy Brand Charcoal, though. In addition, some industries make carbon explicitly intended for agricultural use, such as Tropospheric Coal.

Of example, if you have access to hardwood, it's not that hard to make your own charcoal. In fact, for agricultural use, you don't even need hardwood — just any old vegetable matter — and you can produce charcoal that is now trendy to be called "biochar." The benefits of biochar mixed in soil are numerous and were first found by people living in the Amazon basin in pre-Columbian times. They found that converting their vegetable matter into charcoal, pulverizing it, and applying it to the soil improved the productivity of the soil. Soil scientists have now discovered that carbon dioxide, historically believed to be harmless in soil, reduces soil acidity; provides a refuge for beneficial bacteria live in symbiosis with the root hairs of crops; helps to hold fertilizers in the soil instead of enabling them to be washed away, thereby minimizing the need for fertilizer; and helps to loosen tight soils.

In fact, it tends to sequester emissions from the atmosphere, thereby reducing global warming. Further opportunities have been found all the time.

The three-toned cultivator is a workhorse for elevated beds.

The best way to apply this amazing fertilizer to your garden beds is to get it right where you want it to be used: in your gardens. Using a hoe to make a pair of one-foot-wide and six-to nine-inch-deep trenches running along the length of the room. Place the dry buds, leaves, and other vegetables loosely, but not too closely lined, in the trenches. Then, in a few cases, set them on fire. (Avoid using additives such as charcoal cleaner or fuel because such could severely poison the soil.) When the substance is well burnt and the smoke has turned brown, cover with the mounded soil on the sides of the trenches to rob it of oxygen and let it smolder until the bits are not larger than the card deck. Then, douse the embers with plenty of water. When you do this every fall with garden waste and other vegetable matter, you will soon have soil that, taken along with the other activities here, will have an incredible degree of productivity.

Cover Crops and Helpful Microbes

Today we learn a lot more than our ancestors did about the interaction between plants and soil microorganisms. It points out that soil microorganisms are not only important for the control of pathogens, but are also an essential part of the root structure of the plant. 11 Up to 40% of the carbohydrates provided by plants by photosynthesis are eventually transferred to the root system and out into the soil to feed microorganisms across the root system. Such microorganisms, in effect, expand the root system of the plant and make the required nutrients available.

Friendly microorganisms develop into roots themselves, create mutually beneficial cooperation (symbiosis) and respond to the natural development of antibiotics when required to defend their host. Planting cover crops may help to keep these critters safe during the winter months and shielded from environmental threats such as sunshine and erosion. This way, they're safe and well fed for the next planting season. For these purposes, harvesting should be viewed as a two-part cycle in which the task of harvesting cover crops, which may also be known as green manures, is performed as soon as possible. Green manures are plants cultivated primarily for their function in maintaining soil productivity, but they also reduce deforestation and feed beneficial microbes during the growing season.

The effects of green manure on crop production are far from abstract. For one test, for example, the use of hairy vetch (common legume) as green manure and mulch raised tomato yields by more than 100 per cent.12 Green manures are usually either grains or legumes; grains because of their ability to extract nutrients from a depth of several feet to the surface of the soil,13 and legumes because of their ability to draw nitrogen out of the air and replace it in nodules in t. These are either planted straight into the soil after they have been grown or attached to the compost piles. Legumes use their accumulated nitrogen to produce seeds, and when used as green manures, they need to be cut only before or after flowering. During the summer growing season, green manures will be grown in beds supplemented by heavy-feeding plants, such as cabbage, as part of the crop rotation programme.

Cover Crops / Green Manures and Nitrogen Yields

The use of green manures to provide and improve soil fertility and increased reliance on imported fertilizers is an important aspect of making a mini-farm economically viable. To this end, cover crops should be cultivated during the winter to start the spring compost pile and planted in any bed not in use to avoid nitrogen leaching and encourage higher fertility. Careful use of green manures as cover crops and as different components of compost will fully reduce the need for outside nitrogen inputs.

For eg, alfalfa makes excellent green manure during the growing season, leaving 42 per cent of its nitrogen in the soil when removed, plus adding bio-fixed nitrogen to the compost pile. I propose that 25 to 35 per cent of the growing area of the mini-farm be sown in green manure during the growing season, and that everything be sown in green manure and/or protected in winter. Green manures interplanted with crops during the growing season can create a living mulch. Examples include sowing hairy vetch between corn stalks in the last cultivation before harvesting or planting vegetables without tilling into a bed of already growing subterranean clover.

Hairy vetch is a really good cover crop. Cover crops are not a cure-all, so they will create problems if used indiscriminately. Of example, having a vetch cover crop before growing lettuce can create problems with a lettuce disease called sclerotin.15 Because additional organic matter from the cover crop can create a short-term rise in populations of other pests, such as cutworms, it is necessary to cut or till the cover crop three to four weeks before planting the crops.

Legume green manures, such as peas, beans, etc. In spite of these complexities, how does a farmer pick a cover crop? Cover crops ought to be cultivated on the basis of the environment, the crop to be planted subsequently, and particular factors related to the cover crop, such as its ability to turn into invasive weeds. Legumes and grains are often, but not always, sown together as a cover crop. Many grains, such as oats and wheat, can also act as fruit. If this is expected, it may be worth exploring quickly harvested grains such as hull-less oats. Bear in mind, however, that the option of green manures is at least partially determined by the environment. Many crops that grow well during the winter in South Carolina do not fit in Vermont.

Crop rotation

Crop rotation is one of the oldest and most important farming activities in history and is also one of the most successful in managing the insect population, improving soil fertility and preventing diseases. The primary key to effective crop rotation is to recognize that crops belong to a variety of different botanical families and that members of each related family have specific requirements and pest problems that vary from those of members of other botanical families. For starters, cabbage and brussel sprouts are part of the same botanical family, and they can be expected to have similar soil requirements and to be susceptible to the same pest and disease problems.

Peas and beans are both members of the same botanical family; corn belongs to another family unrelated to the other two. A description of the botanical names of the most grown plant families with edible members is as follows: Amaryllidaceae — leek, common onion, multiplier tomato, tomato, shallot, garlic, chips Brassicaceae — horseradish, mustard, turnip, rutabaga, kale, radish, broccoli, cauliflower, cabbage, collar, Chenopodiaceae — beet, mangel, Swiss chard, lamb quarters, quinoa, spinach Compositae — endive, e. Those results can be partly offset by the use of interference to cover crops between main crops.

Fortunately, a great deal of work has been done on this subject, and while no one is aware of all the factors involved, some general principles have arisen from the study. Always substitute a crop with another crop from the same botanical family (e.g. do not imitate tomato potatoes or cucumber squash). Alternate deep-rooted crops (like carrots) with shallow-rooted crops (like lettuce). Alternate plants that prevent germination (like rye and sunflower) with vegetables but do not interact well with weeds (like peas and strawberries). Alternate crops that contain organic matter (e.g. wheat) to crops that contribute less organic matter (e.g. soybeans). Alternate nitrogen binders (such as alfalfa or vetch) for nitrogen users (such as wheat or vegetables).

The most significant concept for crop rotations is to practice and maintain proper records. Many plant families have a negative impact on other families that can accompany them in succession, but not on others. Such results will vary depending on the method of cropping, manure and composting, meaning that no clear and quick rules apply, so it is almost certain that the farmer can see a difference between the cabbage that follows carrots and the cabbage that follows potatoes.

Keeping careful notes and making minor changes from year to year while monitoring the results would allow the farmer to fine-tune practices aimed at maximizing quality and yield. A three-bed rotation specific to where I live in New Hampshire can give you an idea of how crop rotation with cover crop rotation works. We're going to continue with the drops.

## Chapter Five
## Compost

Whenever you drive through a forest or a long empty area, you see lots of plants even though it's pretty clear that nobody is fertilizing the landscape. Forests and fields do not require fertilizer because they operate within the context of a balanced nitrogen cycle that returns nutrients to the soil by natural composting. The tree absorbs the nutrients from the soil and transforms them into leaves that turn brown and fall to the ground in autumn, creating a sheet on top of last year's leaves. Moving down the rows, just a few centimeters, the leaves turned into a sweet-smelling, breathing compost. It is incorporated into the current soil by the action of earthworms and other species.

The same method is used as the squirrel bites the acorn and lowers the shell to the forest floor and then relieves itself. It all blends in the forest floor so that everything goes back to where it came from and is usable for re-use. Even after death, the same is real. The squirrel eaten by the hawk has all its parts, in some way or another, recycled to the soil; similarly, a massive tree struck by lightning decomposes into the ground for re-use. Life is now prepared to support itself, as it has been for billions of years. Getting energy only from the sun, nature follows the Law of Conservation of Matter to recover all the elements that it receives from the earth.

The method does not operate within a given area of land unless the elements are withdrawn from that area quicker than they can be replaced by removing the elements from elsewhere. It is where the conventional agricultural gangs consider themselves. They sell all their fertility from their farms in the form of seeds and then replenish their fertility with artificial pesticides or fertilizer from other countries. Such a machine will last for a long time, but it is very costly and better suited to large-scale operations. Smaller-scale home-sized projects work less expensively as any attempt is taken to preserve as much soil fertility as possible from sources inside the operation. Aware exposure to the nutrient cycles of the mini-farm will make a big difference in crop yields and the amount of extraneous improvements and fertilizers that need to be introduced — which, in realistic terms, means lower costs.

The fertilizer cycles of the mini-farm include the life-death-birth of plants and animals, as well as the growth-eat-excrete-growth of plants and animals on the farm. The mini-farmer uses composting and nitrogen crops to improve the normal progression of these processes in order to preserve a high degree of soil fertility. The value of compost in a mini-farm or even a small garden can not be overstated. Broadly speaking, compost is the rotting remains of plant and animal materials and by-products that have been aerobically decomposed in such a manner that the actual constituents can not be separated. This is just what's going on in nature, and the minifarmer actually helps the cycle along. If this has happened, the resultant commodity should become agriculturally indispensable. Compost not only acts as a growth buffer due to the individual elements and nutrients it provides, it also helps to kill plant and animal pathogens and contaminants while enhancing the structure and moisture management of the soil to which it is attached. One commercial vegetable grower in California was able to minimize the use of pesticides by 80 per cent in just three years by adding compost. The composting process The basic method of composting is simply this: the farmer stacks up a bunch of organic matter which, with time, air and moisture, decomposes. Fresh content includes table leftovers, farm litter, lawn clippings, leaves raked in the autumn, and animal manure. Essentially, something that was either once alive or created by something that was alive.

A mixture of elements is responsible for organic decomposition, but most importantly microorganisms such as bacteria and fungi that are already found in soil, in plants and also in the intestines of animals. When an ecosystem is produced that is hospitable for growth and reproduction, the microorganisms ingest the organic material. Along with this, a variety of larger organisms, such as earthworms, are in the process of digesting organic matter, thereby producing a entirely new material than what occurred in the first place. Microorganisms, like humans, have different food and habitat habits. Some tend to eat grass, some choose to eat wood, some choose to eat apples. As a result, the highest degree of decomposition and fertility is attributed to the introduction of a number of organic compounds to the mound.

Microorganisms are similarly competitive. -- species (and even the derivative of a given species) needs to make room for itself and its offspring. As a result, many microorganisms have produced a range of weapons that can be used against other microbes in the compost pile. The most commonly known is the development of antibiotics by a number of species engineered to prevent the growth of certain species. Heat-loving bacteria in a compost pile are trying to heat the surface to a high enough degree that other bacteria can't withstand heat and die off. Yet after their research is done, mesophilic bacteria step back into the pile and take over again, along with the fungi and eventually the earthworms.

Composting to Death Pathogens

Microorganisms that create compost can be loosely categorized as either thermophilic — meaning "hot loving "— or mesophilic — meaning" intermediate loving "— both words relating to the temperatures desired by and generated by these microorganisms. The compost pile is alluded to as either thermophilic or mesophilic based on the temperature it reaches. Pathogen mortality is the most important part of the ambient temperatures of the compost pile. Thermophilic composting kills all known human pathogens — including parasitic worm larvae, fungi, viruses and protozoa — along with plant disease species and weed seeds.

Using thermophilic composting, it is also feasible and realistic to recycle not just ordinary plant material such as leaves and grass clippings, but even left over fried chicken. In other words, thermophilic composting allows a much wider variety of compost materials both functional and safe. There are two causes causing the mortality in compost of plant or animal pests and herb seeds. The temperature of the compost, as described above, is a major factor. Another significant aspect is the time the compost is processed before it is used. Microbial pathogens need different hosts to complete their life cycles, and their spores will stay inert — and therefore viable — only in a dry, moist compost pile for so long. Even if the compost pile is not thermophilic, the proper keeping time would also make the compost both secure and profitable. Weed seeds can be destroyed by the high heat of the thermophilic compost pile, but they can also be destroyed by the fact that the temperature of such a mesophilic pile can cause premature germination, thus interrupting the life cycle of the weeds.

Mesophylic compost retention time is two years whether it contains or is expected to contain bacteria from contaminated seeds, dead animals or other materials. Thermophilic compost containing any of more of these items just needs to be stored for a year. Compost made entirely from non-disease-infected plants may be used after six months, irrespective of the temperature of the mound. Some home composting books and publications include lengthy lists of items not to be composted, and the list includes diseased vegetables, meat waste, peanut butter, cooking oils, carnivorous or omnivorous feces, and so on. Such a list of forbidden products makes good sense when working with mesophilic compost (or meeting organic certification standards), particularly if it is not kept for a few years to insure pathogen death — and most home composting is mesophilic. So by using thermophilic composting, the number of forbidden items will go into the compost pile, and you can recycle all of your leftovers.

Thermophilic Composting

Four factors are required to achieve thermophilic composting: sufficient bulk, sufficient aeration, adequate moisture and a suitable ratio of carbon to nitrogen, known as the C / N ratio. Composing methods are typically defined as either batch methods or continuous methods. Batch methods add all components at once, while continuous methods slowly add to the stock. Through nature, most mini-farmers and home gardeners are continuous composters. As a result, the early stages of the compost pile do not have enough mass to sustain heat from thermophilic composting. This dilemma can be overcome by timing: start fresh compost piles in the morning, so that by the time the weather is chilly, the pile still has plenty of bulk to keep warm during the winter.

During the season, not only do you replace the leaves that fell on the yard during the autumn, but you also add the new manures that were grown in the autumn for the season harvest and add them to the pile as well. You may also add livestock manure (if available) and any grass clippings or other crop debris. It is going to get the pile off to a strong start with a lot of weight. If the leaves are not usable, straw or hay would fit just as well. The different materials are applied to the pile in alternating layers not more than two inches deep, ensuring that lawn clippings or leaves are not matted down to create a crust that is impermeable to the air.

If you end up with a layer a bit too deep, don't worry, because the next time you change the compost over, all the layers will be mixed up. Aeration is important because thermophilic composting is aerobic and requires oxygen. There are two groups of microorganisms involved in the decomposition of organic materials — aerobic microorganisms that work in the presence of oxygen, and anaerobic microorganisms that work in the absence of oxygen. Aerobic composting removes or prevents odors and makes thermophilic bacteria, whereas anaerobic composting smells like a septic tank and never produces a lot of moisture. Aeration is therefore necessary in order to make good compost and preserve peace in the neighbourhood. Aeration is accomplished by rotating and combining compost piles on a daily basis. The idea of transforming compost is so ingrained that a number of businesses are now making costly devices to help people turn around and break down their compost.

Drilled PVC pipe for compost aeration. So much compost recycling is counterproductive and can potentially be counter-productive by creating a lack of both essential nitrogen and organic matter. It can also help to dissipate any heat by turning a compost pile. The solution to the dilemma is to create the compost pile in such a manner that it is self-aerating. This is done by layering the straw as you go along — just have a few bales ready next to the compost pile. By inserting a sheet of straw and making sure that no sheet in the stack of any given ingredient is more than a few inches thick without being split up by either straw or some other ingredient, a self-aerating stack is guaranteed. Alternatively, you can try my system by which large-diameter PVC pipes with holes drilled in them are buried vertically in the pile.

Not all batteries may be installed in a way that ensures self-aeration, of course; in these situations it is completely important to crank the pile up to five times a year. In addition, if the pile is not self-aerating, it should be turned on a regular basis. After sustained heavy rains that can suck up the pile and push out the air, turning is a smart idea. In addition, a lot of water is used in the composting process, so when compost is processed, water can be applied if needed.

It's important to water the pile as it moves. Adequate ventilation is another essential aspect of composting. Too much moisture in compost drives out of the soil, contributing to anaerobic decomposition, which is not thermophilic and almost always smells unpleasant. Too little moisture in soil allows microorganisms to go dormant or to function less efficiently. Thankfully, the optimal amount for compost is generally very flexible and can be anything between 40 percent to 60 percent, so all that is needed is for any dry layers applied to the pile (such as leaves or sawdust) to be dampened with a hose if there is no rain in the forecast. Some extra moisture needed will be provided by rain in much of North America.

Extremely wet climates that require that the pile be covered with tarp on occasion, and drought conditions may demand that the pile be inspected and water added if the moisture content is not that of a wrung-out sponge. Note, again, that when compost is processed, check to see if water is needed, and if necessary, add it. Much like humans need nutrients to be most competitive at a given stage, microorganisms responsible for composting have dietary needs. The most important dietary criterion for microbes in the manufacture of thermophilic compost is the ratio of carbon to nitrogen in the plant. Microbes require nitrogen to produce proteins, so they need carbon for nearly everything. The carbon-nitrogen ratio of 30:1 should result in thermophilic compost.22 This ratio should not be practiced slavishly. Microbes are picky, but they're not that picky. Anywhere from 35:1 to 25:1 is going to work perfectly. The proper carbon / nitrogen ratio can be obtained by combining materials with higher and lower C / N ratios in approximate proportions. For eg, cow manure with a C / N ratio of 20:1 can be combined with oak leaves with a C / N ratio of 50:1 to obtain the optimal ratio of 30:1. Perhaps more quickly, half-and-a-half green vegetable waste combined with dry vegetable waste can yield the same effect.

Carbon to Nitrogen Ratios of Commonly Composted Materials
Material Vegetable wastes

Ratio 12-20:1

Alfalfa hay 13:1

Cow manure 20:1

Leaves 40-80:1

Corn stalks 60:1

Oat straw 74:1

Wheat straw 80:1

Sawdust 100-500:1

Grass clippings 12-25:1

Coffee grounds 20:1

Poultry manure 10:1

Horse manure 25:1

When a compost pile is built, and it just doesn't seem to heat up, test the moisture and add water or drain as appropriate, then poke the holes deep within it with the aeration rod. If none of these works is needed, nitrogen must be added. Ideally, this will be achieved by adding in green grass, but blood meal combined with water and poured in aeration holes would also work. Blood meal is growing and can be purchased from garden shops and possibly nearby Walmart shops. When my batteries don't heat up the way they can because of a lack of nitrogen, all I do is apply a regular organic nitrogen-containing fertilizer and a touch of compost activator any time I turn them on. A soil and/or compost thermometer can be bought easily so that you can measure the efficiency of your layer. You want the battery to hit a limit of 130 to 160 degrees for no less than 15 days. For fact, it is unlikely that the compost will survive at this temperature for 15 days in a row. You can tell when the temperature begins to decrease by using a thermometer.

Mix the stack carefully any time you see the temperature decrease, and after a few days, the stack will heat up again if the moisture level is right. This way, you will get at least 15 days of thermophilic temperatures in your compost. At thermophilic compost temperatures of 140 degrees, roundworm and other eggs are killed within two hours or less, and most other protozoa, bacteria, and viruses are killed within minutes. The most dangerous germ is salmonella, which is destroyed in only 20 hours. By having 15 days at temperatures above 130 degrees Celsius, you produce manure that is completely healthy to add to crops that enter the surface, virtually without regard to the ingredients.

Compost Aging

Both temperatures and preservation periods have an effect on the removal of bacteria, along with the biochemistry of the compost layer. In the case of a pile made from non-diseased plants and manures, a long retention period is not needed to ensure that the compost is hygienic, but a minimum retention period is certainly necessary to insure that the compost is healthy. Immature compost may produce phytotoxins that slow germination and can use nutrients from any bed to which it is attached.

The guidelines of the Canadian Council of Ministers of the Environment state that six months is adequate processing period for compost, and it works if composting has been mesophilic or thermophilic as long as diseased materials have not been used. If disease species are likely to be present (because contaminants from contaminated crops or meat products have been added), then compost will be kept for one year if thermophilically composted and for two years otherwise.

Proper ageing of the compost can be checked without a expensive laboratory using radish seeds, since the radishes are highly susceptible to phytotoxins in immature compost. Buy a commercial seed-starter combination, dampen it and growing it in a seed-starting tub. Place the compost to be checked in another container in the same setting as the first one, then plant 20 radish seeds on each surface. Wash both on a daily basis, and held at 70 degrees F. Look at the germination. When the germination rate of the seeds in the compost is less than 80% of that of the conventional seed-starter mix, the compost has to mature a little more.

Compost Activators

Nearly every gardening publication has ads in the back for so-called compost activators. Usually, these materials contain a mixture of bacteria and fungi that support the composting cycle. Although these items would definitely not harm your compost, they are usually not necessary either, since the compost activators are free all around you. The last year's compost and healthy garden soil are the two most effective compost activators. They produce a variety of sufficient bacterial and fungal spores that will seed your collection. Just a shovel or two of these blended into the pile is necessary periodically.

A few commercial compost activator devices are tested and noticed little difference between the piles in which they were used and the piles in which they were not used — except in situations where the pile failed to heat up sufficiently due to lack of moisture. In such situations, the addition of the activator mixed in with the added water raises the rate at which the battery heats up. The Grow Biointensive system of composting — a mesophilic process — specifies that 1/3 of the final weight of the compost will be from the garden soil.

The reason for this is that it leaves the compost pile "cold" so that it composts slowly. This has the advantage of retaining more organic matter and more nitrogen as the thermophilic process is never reached. I can not refute this profit, but I do not support this method because the advantages of thermophilic composting — removing disease species and having a broader variety of compost ingredients — compete with a marginally higher loss of organic matter. So use a garden soil shovel or last year's compost as an activator, just don't get carried away or you'll end up with compost that won't hit high enough temperatures to destroy disease species.

Plant covers fall crops that are harvested in the spring and used to create a thermophilic compost pile when mixed with grass, straw and other high-carbon materials. Add organic household waste including food leftovers to the bin, along with any available animal manures. Using straw or sawdust as a cover layer before adding something that will attract dogs or rats or hide them deeply in the mound. Add field debris in the fall and a decent layer of hay or straw on top for the season. In the spring, start a second pile, and leave the first one sit for a year to heal, because uncured compost will harm soil fertility; requiring a year to heal often ensures hygienic compost. The first pile is ready for use the next season.

Three-bin composting system of the founder. If a potentially pathogenic substance has been composted or the compost has never reached a thermophilic level, it is better to keep the compost for a few years and make sure it is healthy.

## Chapter Six
## Plant nutrients in-depth

Plants produce their own vitamins, which is one of the reasons that they are so healthy. Yet to produce them, or occasionally just to survive, they require a wide variety of macronutrients and micronutrients. Most micronutrients take care of themselves by using different compost materials, specifically adding kelp or seaweed to compost once and a while, if usable, and using commercial liquid kelp fertilizers such as Neptune's Harvest or Root Boost and beds. In spite of this, shortcomings still grow. In my greenhouse, where I grow a lot of cabbage-family plants, boron can be a specific concern, because with inadequate boron, broccoli grows with hollow stems. And I precisely apply a tablespoon of borax (mixed with a cup of blood meal for quick dispersion) to every garden bed at the beginning of each gardening season.

These hollow stems are the product of boron deficiency.

Macronutrients

Calcium: activates rhizobia bacteria, is essential to stable cell walls, assists in the transport of carbohydrates inside plants, aids in the digestion of trace elements and facilitates the development of enzymes. Adequate calcium (or even uptake) is required to avoid potato scab, blossom end rot, black carrot lesions, and other diseases. Adding lime (which provides calcium) to the hole when transplanting brassica will help avoid a fungal disease called "club foot." Bioavailable calcium is essential for the proper use of nitrogen. Plants use significant quantities of calcium, which is why it is important to maintain adequate levels in the soil.

Some of the time, this is achieved by applying various kinds of lime. Calcium may be applied in the form of standard garden lime; dolomitic limestone, which also includes magnesium; and pulverized oyster shells. We all need time to grow to become bioavailable, and I usually consider bringing them to beds in the fall so that they have time to work before the garden season begins in the spring. In fact, you can add 8 pounds of lime a year to every 100 square feet of garden beds. I usually consider using dolomitic lime as magnesium and calcium to work together in a manner that supports plants.

Nitrogen: Nitrogen is an important element of life because, combined with carbon and hydrogen, it is a building block for amino acids which combine to create proteins and even the basic data of life: RNA and DNA. Nitrogen is essential to the metabolic cycle in a plant and to the production of valuable compounds such as chlorophyll. Plants like a lot of water, unsurprisingly. In the previous portion, we discussed nitrogen sources and amounts. Phosphorus: Phosphorus is an ingredient in cellular protoplasm and is essential for both cell division and development. It is the single most essential factor for the germination and development of plants, followed soon by nitrogen.

Almost all soils are deficient and need to be supplemente. The most apparent position where phosphorous deficiency is noticeable is in seedlings, as the beginning medium is normally nutrient deficient. On these cases, the leaves grow a purplish tint on the underside. In the case of seedlings, a full liquid fertilizer containing phosphorus, such as Neptune's Harvest (if growing organically) or Miracle Gro, will otherwise go off at the edge. Apply fertilizer to seedlings after the first collection of leaves emerges and every two weeks thereafter by using a nutrient-free growing medium.

Potassium: plants need a broad and continuous supply of potassium to support the digestion and transport of carbohydrates, protein synthesis, growth and cell division. Adequate supplies of potassium ensure improved appearance, colour and taste of vegetables and fruit. The key sign of deficiency can be seen in the leaf edges which tend to be "scorched." Root crops, in particular, need sufficient potassium and maybe even higher levels for better growth. Chapter 4 provides detail on the correct potassium levels to be preserved in your beds.

Micronutrients

Boron: Although categorized as a micronutrient due to the limited amount needed, it is completely essential to nearly all plant life processes, including hormonal development, ion exchange, nutrient movement and water metabolism. Each plant displays boron deficiency a little differently, based on the severity. The beans are deformed in the shells. The roots in the broccoli are hollow. Since deficiency symptoms can easily be associated with deficiencies in other components, the best option, outside of a qualified soil check, is to ensure sufficient supplies on a daily basis. Since excess boron can be poisonous to plants, and plants can consume excess boron if there is too much available, you need to be careful to use just what is required. You should add three teaspoons of borax per 100 square feet of bed space once a year, and this will usually work perfectly. You will blend it thoroughly with something like lime powder or bone meal before transmitting to ensure even delivery, and then push it into the top few inches of soil.

Copper: Copper plays an important function in root metabolism, photosynthesis and enzyme activation, as well as in shielding plants from the harmful effects of excess nitrogen. Copper, like boron, is needed in very small amounts and is toxic in abundance. It is available in the form of copper sulfate crystals which should be added to beds annually at a rate of 1-1/2 ounces (four tablespoons) per 100 square feet of space. As it is difficult to spread such a limited amount uniformly over such a wide area, it should be thoroughly combined with anything to be applied to beds in greater amounts, such as lime, bone meal, or other fertilizer. Iron: While needed in very limited amounts, iron is necessary for the chlorophyll cycle in plants. Without it, plants tend to become "bleached out" (called chlorosis) and suffer from stunted development. Toxicity is not a major iron problem, as plants prefer to self-regulate how much they take out of the soil.

However, if only small quantities are needed, the excess should not be given. By the way, iron can be applied by the use of blood meal as a nitrogen source. Since I use blood meal in my greenhouse, Iron deficiency has never been a matter of concern. However, others would choose not to use blood meal, in which case it is recommended to add six ounces of iron (or ferric) sulfate per 100 square feet of garden bed per year. Another more sustainable option is to purposely use nettle seeds, which are very rich in iron, in the compost pile.

Magnesium: Magnesium is an essential factor in the whole garden. It speeds up composting, makes nitrogen more readily accessible, activates rhizobia bacteria, improves root growth, and is essential for carbohydrate motility in plants. It works in equilibrium with calcium in a number of ways and eliminates the results that may (however unlikely) occur from unnecessary concentrations of copper, manganese or iron in the soil.

Magnesium coexists with calcium in dolomitic lime, and you will have no trouble with magnesium deficiency as long as you have dolomitic limestone as a source of calcium in your beds. Magnesium sulfate — also known as Epsom salt — is sold in food stores or supermarkets and can be purchased at an average rate of 24 ounces per 100 square feet of garden area.

Manganese: While manganese is only needed sparingly, its existence in adequate amounts can have an enormous positive impact on crop yields, especially for root crops. Deficiency is known as a consistent yellowing of new leaves. This makes sense, since manganese is important to the development of chlorophyll. Most soils have sufficient natural manganese, but if soil pH is higher than 6.5, supplementation may be needed. In fact, overcrowded soils can be deficient. If you believe a deficiency, you should add 12 ounces of manganese sulfate every 100 square feet to your bed once every three years.

Molybdenum: Molybdenum is an important substrate for the production of enzymes and the synthesis of amino acids and proteins. While essential, it is extremely toxic to plants in excess of that. When you mistakenly apply too much molybdenum to your beds, clean them with copper sulfate, which decreases the bioavailability of molybdenum and make it less toxic. Many soils today, including those in agricultural use, are deficient in molybdenum. If you add manganese when molybdenum is still low, it makes matters worse — so consider using molybdenum and manganese together.

Supplementation can be in the form of molybdenum acid, ammonium molybdate or sodium molybdate at a rate of 1-1/2 ounce per 100 square feet of garden bed mixed with something else to allow further use. Molybdenum disulfide, used as a lubricant, is not ideal because it is so solid that it does not have an efficient biological supply. Sulfur: Sulfur is an critical component of the essential amino acids needed for the processing of plant proteins. Essentially, without sulfur, plants cease to exist. At the other hand, sulfur occurs in several different ways, and others are more beneficial to plants than others, while some are entirely poisonous. In addition, the sulfate forms of sulfur are beneficial for plants, while the sulfide forms of sulfur are deleterious.

Since sulfur compounds tend to acidify the soil a bit, you can keep an eye on the soil pH and apply lime if necessary to prepare for the pH effects of sulfur. Sulfur is typically spread in the form of pure elemental sulphur, known as "sulphur flowers." Distribute evenly over beds at a rate of 24 ounces per 100 square feet once a year.

Zinc: Zinc is essential to the growth of crops, the digestion and control of water and carbon dioxide in plants. Zinc deficiency is not especially widespread, but it can be detected in the form of chlorotic bands inside the leaves of the plant when it occurs. Zinc is much more available in acidic soils (pH less than 7) than in alkaline soils (pH greater than 7). Thus, if the soil in the beds were alkaline, the 12 ounces of zinc sulfate per 100 square feet of bed required to fix or avoid deficiency will have to be multiplied by five for a minimum of 60 ounces.

Creating a Micronutrient Balance

After the mini-farm has been up and running for three years or so, this is likely to be redundant for existing beds as soil fertility activities can retain a lot of plant nutrients. But, if you just get going, it may be needed. With maximum of 300 square feet, add the following ingredients in a bowl and dry mix thoroughly: Borax: 1-1/2 oz. Copper sulfate: 4-1/2 oz.

Ferric sulfate: 18 oz. Magnesium sulfate: 72 oz. Manganese sulfate: 12 oz. Sodium molybdate: 4-1/2 oz. Sulfate: 36 oz. Zinc sulfate: 36 oz. The main explanation is that the biochar in the soil retains nutrients so that they do not spill, the use of cover crops prevents nutrients from shifting, and the careful composting of all plant matter from the field maintains the nutrients that have reached the plants from the soil so that they can be returned to the soil. Another factor is the number of inputs. I use a lot when I use synthetic fertilizers.

For potassium, I can use greensand at the beginning of the season, then wood ashes at the end. And all over the house, the compost bin gathers a wide variety of items, ranging from seed debris and grass clippings to rotten eggs and the bowels of slaughtered animals. As a result, since the cattle are mostly fed from the crop, the manure contains more nutrients than was originally withdrawn from the earth, rendering it an excellent fertilizer. This is really significant. Anything that you can't produce or save on your mini-farm will ultimately cost you money. Holding costs down is the trick that makes mini-farming an economic practice more profitable than mere gardening.

## Chapter Seven
## Time and yield

Most of the United States, including the northern plains, has a growing season long enough to require several plantings of several crops. In fact, well-organized scheduling enables harvesting to be scheduled either to allow harvesting for everyday use or selling at a time — which is useful for crops such as lettuce — or to allow frequent large-scale harvesting for conservation and storage purposes. Many crops are frost-hardy, so the second planting would allow the harvest to continue for as long as a month after the first fall frost, without doing anything to extend the season. For example, two broccoli or spinach crops can be grown in the same area as one crop, doubling production per unit area.

Succession Planting This is a strategy to increase the productivity of the garden area by making a new crop ready to be planted as soon as an earlier crop is harvested. An example is the planting of a second broccoli crop in the same region where the first broccoli crop was harvested in midsummer. One example is the early sowing of spinach and then the planting of beans where the spinach used to be as soon as the spinach was picked. Crops that perform well for early planting in succession are all from the family of cabbage, spinach, peas, radishes, turnips, beets and onions. ('Sets' are small onions for planting that you can purchase in a mesh bag in the garden center. They're not the same as store onions.) The above-mentioned crops are usually harvested no later than mid-July. Crops that can be planted in mid-July for late summer or fall harvest include bush beans, lettuce, spinach, carrots, turnips, beets, parsnips and everything in the cabbage family.


Timed Planting Timed Planting involves spacing the harvest by amazing the planting dates for a single crop over a few weeks rather than planting it all at once. The consequence is a constant supply of a single product for the market or a persistent harvest that can be fried, consumed or canned in short sessions. The best way to do so is to take the total number of plants expected for the crop and split it by three. Sow the first third on the first sowing day for that seed, the second third a week after, and the final third two weeks after. This will result in the same overall yield as planting the whole crop at once, it will spread the yield over a two-week period. Replanting is the next element of accelerated planting. Take carrots, for example; if carrots were planted in four sessions, every two weeks apart, after the first planting is harvested, the field might be replanted with more carrots so that the field would never be idle. Once the last carrot crop is primed for harvest, you are just two weeks out from your first harvest. Succession planting and accelerated planting also have a little protection, because if the weather is extreme, sooner or later, there's always a crop. What you need to learn for productive succession and/or timed planting is the days to maturity of the crop under consideration and its frost hardness.

Inter-planting

Inter-planting is used in two different ways. This is used to give the green manures a head start in the winter and to increase the amount of grain that can be harvested from a given field. Carefully selected, inter-planted crops may also save on fertilizer, as where a nitrogen source, such as beans or clover, is inter-planted with a nitrogen recipient, such as tomatoes or corn. There are some logistical drawbacks of Inter-planting, and the main of these is overcrowding and shadow. Plants that need a lot of space or sunshine, such as tomatoes, may have trouble planting in an existing corn stand. If they were planted before the corn had germinated, the tomatoes would shade the seedlings. On the other side, white clover fits best with most seeds, much like beans.

The Inter-planting of crops produces synergies. Perhaps the most prominent example of good Inter-planting is the so-called Three Sisters of the Native Americans — corn, beans, and squash that they grew together. In this situation, the pole beans and the squash vines used the protection of the corn stalks.

Fall Planting

Frost hardy crops and biennials kept alive through the winter for seed development (called "overwintering") can be first planted in the spring, then harvested in the summer, and then replanted for the second autumn or early winter harvest. Late harvesting can be done for certain crops without the challenge of using seasonal extension systems. Overwintering seeds, so that they can be used either when required or for seed growth, is more troublesome. This can be performed outside in the South or Pacific Northwest. In the upper Midwest or Northeast, these plants must be taken indoors for the winter or, at the very least, covered by a cold or unheated greenhouse.

Regarding the purposes of autumn planting, crops may be classified into three categories: mild, semi-hardy and hardy. Tender crops are damaged by mild frosts. Semi-hardy crops will withstand soft frosts and hardy crops should withstand hard frosts. The best bets for autumn planting are semi-hard and hardy varieties. Many hardy vegetables, such as broccoli and spinach, also taste best when cultivated in the fall rather than in the spring. Semi-hardy crops should be scheduled for harvest within 28 days after the first frost, and hardy crops should be harvested within 56 days after the first frost. The time to harvest must be understood for this. -- crop variety has slightly different maturity dates, and these dates are shown in the seed catalogs and in the seed packets. As the development is slower in the fall, 10 days will be added to the maturity period, so plant 10 days sooner for the fall harvest.

Crop Hardiness Tender Beans

- Semi-hard beet
- Hardy Broccoli
- corn
- carrot
- Brussels Sprouts
- cucumber
- cauliflower
- cabbage
- eggplant
- celery
- Kale
- melon
- beet
- onion
- Okra
- lettuce
- parsley
- pepper

- Parsnip
- pea
- squash
- potato
- spinach
- sweet potato
- turnip
- tomato

Using Seedlings for a Head Start

Some vegetables, such as cucumbers, may be cultivated or grown directly in the greenhouse. Transplanting seedlings gives the plant a head start which will encourage optimum output from the number of growing days in the season. Winter squash, taking 80 or more days to harvest, is a good candidate for planting seedlings, especially in the northern half of the United States, where there are sometimes less than 90 frost-free days in a row during the growing season. Since squash will not be immediately planted until 14 days after the last freeze, leaving fewer than 80 available growing days, growing transplants would then maximize the amount of squash harvested without allowing the farmer to use seasonal extension equipment. The same refers to crops in the fall garden. Throughout the late season, broccoli may be planted immediately, but giving it a four-week head start by developing indoor seedlings and then transplanting them can accelerate harvesting. Another area where you can use this approach to a positive purpose is a crop that most writers would warn you not to transplant: maize.

Produced on the agribusiness scale, sweet corn seed is usually covered with a fungicide to prevent it from rotting in the dirt. Crop corn is susceptible not only to rot, but to be consumed by wire worms. Besides, not all of them germinate at the same time. It's all out on a very wide scale. But it can be a issue on a small scale — say, growing 48 plants in a 4-foot × 8-foot raised bed. Transplanting of seedlings is the perfect approach. What I am doing is starting 64 seedlings indoors around two weeks before the first frost-free date. It's important not to try for longer than two weeks, because the corn grows taproot, and after that, the transplant shock may be too high. Following two weeks, others may not have germinated, and others may be taller than others. All I do is pick the 48 most standardized plants and move them to the bed.

For a week, you can keep the others handy only in case of worm cuts or related pest attacks. You will use this method on most crops except root crops. Starting from seed indoors, you achieve an edge anywhere from two to six weeks. For Timeline The following table is part of a calendar for my own Own Hampshire mini-farm, so the exact dates do not fit for you. However, the explanations given will be helpful.

# Chapter Eight
## Watering and irrigation

It is necessary to ensure that crops have the right amount of water without overwatering them. Properly irrigated crops are more resistant to pests, consume nutrients more easily and are usually stronger and more productive. While it is possible to water crops a little everyday, such an method poses problems. As one thing, if enough water is not used to penetrate deep into the soil, the roots of the plants would stick close to the surface, rendering it difficult for the farmer to miss irrigation for a few days. A safer solution to water is incredibly detailed, but less regular. "Thorough" watering is equal to one inch of rain, which is equal to around five pints of water per square foot of a garden area. In regular conditions, this volume of water will be absorbed down into the soil so that plant roots can be well formed, and irrigation will only be needed once a week or twice a week during excessively hot weather.

Garden soil, when dry, is initially repelled by water. When the water is actually pumped to the surface, the stream will flow to the lowest level it will reach and the pool there before it is drained. Have the soil a bit moist first, and it's going to suck up water like a sponge. There are as many ways to gardening as there are gardeners. The Square Foot system uses a ladle to water every square foot of a raised bed individually. The reason for this is not only the lack of water, but the fact that preventing vegetation from becoming wet helps avoid disease problems.

This is real, but the question lies in the fact that such a form of watering is burdensomely time-consuming when performed on a scale of just a few hundred square feet. The Grow Biointensive approach imitates natural rainfall by using special watering attachments that create tiny droplets which enable the water to fall with just the force of gravity. By watering thoroughly every time, the amount of watering is kept at around once a week. It is much less time-consuming than watering each square foot separately, and since it is watering regularly rather than constantly, it is easier than routine disease-based watering regimens, but not as effective as the Square Foot system in that respect. Agriculture, like everything else, needs cooperation! All else being fair, using a watering wand is the safest strategy for a mini-farmer in the first few years.

Usage of a irrigation wall

A irrigation wand may be used to mimic normal rainfall. It is worth it, because traditional watering attachments will make the water too strong, causing erosion and destroying seeds and seedlings.

The watering wand makes the distribution of the water at the correct time.Some, but not all, watering wands have a movable head that allows various water flow configurations to be used.

When you have one like this, make sure you pick the "shower" mode. Unfortunately, when watering by hand, it's impossible to say how much water comes in. Luckily, it's easy to find it out. Take a garden hose with a shower watering extension, place it in a five-gallon bucket, and turn it on. (The shower watering device is also known as the "watering wand." Use nothing but a watering wand whether you cool by hand or harm the plants.) Use the second hand sweep on the watch to see how long it takes to fill the tank. If it takes two minutes to fill the tank, you know that the flow rate of the hose and adapter is 2.5 gallons per minute. A 100-square-foot garden bed takes 62 gallons of water a week. By dividing 62 by 2.5, you will discover that by irrigating the bed equally for 25 minutes, you can have ample water. If your farm is something like mine, most of the beds are about 4-foot × 8-foot, or 32 square feet. That's around 1/3 of 100 square feet, and if you split the 62 gallons of water in a 100-square-foot bed by three, you get 20 to 21 gallons of water in a 32-square-foot space. When the connection water is 4 gallons a minute, so that means watering the bed for 5 minutes.

Using the "shower" settings to prevent destroying trees.

Obviously, this is time-consuming. A three-person self-sufficient mini-farm would have more than a few tents, and hand watering would take a lot of time and be pretty boring. One way to prevent monotony is to split the beds so that 1/5 of the beds are watered every day of the week. When you've grown to a broad enough mini-farm for watering chores to take a majority of your energy, you can plan some kind of irrigation network (if possible) to maximize your energy use.

Drip Irrigation

Perhaps the better method in terms of time, quality and disease control is drip irrigation, in which tubes bring water to hidden parts of the garden at a fixed flow rate. It can be expensive to deploy initially, but it pays for itself in the long term by freeing up the resources. One of the best features of drip irrigation systems is that they are compact and use interchangeable fittings, which ensures that a farmer can start small and extend the system slowly as time and finances permit. Drip irrigation offers the advantages of watering each plant separately and leaving the vegetation dry and thereby avoiding diseases thus saving significant time.

Drip irrigation systems are measured in gallons per hour, per foot or per emitter. (The emitter is a small instrument that delivers water from the tank to the plants.) In the case of intensive cultivation, the emitters will be spaced every 6 to 12 inches as the plants grow very closely together. Drip tape is suitable for complex applications and should be placed in the direction of the distributor in such a manner that there is at least one emitter per square foot of the raised bed. An automatic timer can be mounted such that, if the flow rate of the emitters is determined, the time can be adjusted precisely to require the correct volume of water. Hold a weather gage in the garden, and you'll know that the garden has to be sprayed even if there's less than one inch of weather in a week. If the amount of rain that falls is less than one inch, the amount of water (in gallons) required per square foot can be determined using the following formula: $0.62 \times (1-z)$ where z is the number of inches of rain that falls that week.

Soaker Hoses

Not every mini-farmer wants to install a drip irrigation or gray water recycling system. The use of soaker hoses is a reasonable option. Soaker hoses should be laid lengthwise on the top of the garden bed and serpented back and forth so that consecutive runs are no more than one foot apart. Alternatively, no more than four inches thick should be dug in the garden beds. I attempted to insert a soaker hose about eight inches deep in the garden, and because most of the roots of the plant are in the top six inches of dirt, it didn't fit so well. The soaker hoses must be on the surface of the soil or buried no more than four inches deep.

Two common soaker hose types.

The watering speeds of the soaker hoses can vary depending on the manufacturer. One company, manufactured by Fiskars, water at a rate of one gallon an hour an 10 linear feet of hose when attached to a 10 psi pressure regulator. Up to six lengths of soaker hose up to 100 feet in length each can be extended from the same spigot / pressure regulator. The introduction of an automatic timer to the machine makes watering effortless. Calculating how long it takes to turn the soaker on is easy.

One inch of rain on a 100-square-foot garden bed is 62 gallons of water, and this is what is required weekly for optimum plant safety. If well spread out, a 4-foot × 25-foot garden bed will require a 100-foot soaker hose. If the hose waters run at a rate of one gallon per hour per 10 linear feet, so 100 linear feet would be taken out of 10 gallons of water per hour. And, in just six hours, 62 gallons will be shipped. Once a week, when the automatic timer is set to water for six hours, you are free from watering chores except in the case of young seedlings that need to be watered by hand

## Chapter Nine
## Crop proportion and sizing

How much of each crop to produce depends on a variety of factors, but most importantly on your needs and the needs of retail outlets whether you want to produce enough to sell. The percentages are useful for strategic preparation, but nothing else is average. All this means is that no one can make a map telling you precisely when to rise. Folks in the United States are eating notoriously unhealthful foods.

According to the USDA Centre for Nutrition Policy and Promotion, about 10% of Americans have a balanced diet.25 So, before we get into seed proportions and sizes, let's take a quick glance at dietary needs. As of 2006, the USDA Food Pyramid describes the daily servings of various food classes. Through analyzing what constitutes "served" in each case and performing a little multiplication, we will establish a goal amount appropriate for a balanced diet that can be changed later if necessary to accommodate the family's dietary needs and activity rates.

2006 USDA Food Pyramid A serving is a single slice of bread; 1/2 cup of rice, pasta or prepared breakfast cereal; or one ounce of ready-to-eat breakfast cereal. Serving ratios are measured on the basis of 1/2 ounce of flour per meal. Of food, a serving is one cup of green leafy vegetables or half a cup of some other kind of vegetables, whether fresh or fried. Three quarters of a cup of vegetable juice is also a meal. Potatoes are counted as a vegetable, half a cup of which is a meal. Botany describes tomatoes as fruit, but U.S. law describes tomatoes as vegetables. For the benefit of the food pyramid, tomatoes are a vegetable.

A serving of fruit is a medium-sized whole fruit or 1/2 cup of fresh berries or canned / cooked fruit. Three quarters of a cup of fruit juice is also a helping of food. Both kinds of beef, but also of dry beans, eggs and nuts, fall under the category of poultry. 2.5 ounces is a serving with red meat, poultry and seafood. One potato, half a cup of tofu, half a cup of dried beans and 1/4 of a cup of dried seed is a meal. One cup of milk or cream, or 1,5 to 2 ounces of cheese, is a serving of milk. Using the Food Pyramid Guidance and serving sizes, we can set the target production numbers for one person.

Per-Person Yearly Food Requirements Crop

Per-Person Yearly Requirement

Vegetables456 lbs

Fruit365 lbs

Wheat, corn, oats, and rice250 lbs

Total lean meats and eggs 159 lbs

What these figures mean is that the average diet for a family of two adults and one child includes 1,368 pounds of fruits, 1,095 pounds of fruit, 750 pounds of food, and 477 pounds of meat and eggs. This is, of course, subject to dietary tastes and allergies, and no one can tell you whether to produce at the individual crop level. But at the level of gross nutrients, the USDA food pyramid will give you a decent starting point to customize. Different crops yield different yields per unit of land, and a mini-farmer must be mindful of the planned yields for resource allocation preparation.

Non-hybrid plant varieties are believed to have ample water in ordinary soil. The exact yield would depend on the diversity of the crop and the individual growing conditions. And, it is very probable (even likely) that a farmer with a richly composted soil will surpass such yields. Our imaginary family of three (two adults and one teenager) requires 1,368 pounds of vegetables a year. Averaging the yield of different vegetables, you get 220 pounds per 100 square feet of bed space, which ensures that all the vegetable needs of a household can be conveniently covered in 700 square feet of bed space, assuming a variety of vegetables. The same imaginary family wants 1,095 pounds of fruit each year. Mushrooms, cantaloupes, and melons are all counted as fruits. Unfortunately, in most cases, they don't last any longer than the rising season. Crop trees and vines are ideally suited for the production of crop in large amounts. They're not grown in raised beds, then they're grown in the field. A dwarf apple tree can produce up to 160 pounds of fruit each year. Apples fit well in the root cellar and are quickly turned into apple sauce, and dehydrated apples make a delicious addition to the oatmeal. Another good source of fruit is sweet and sour cherries, which yield 300 and 150 pounds of fruit per flower. Blackberry canes are simple and quick to produce, yielding up to 50 pounds of blackberry per 100 square feet. Strawberries can yield about 100 pounds per 100 square feet of land. Any number of fruit combinations could work, but one example that will produce 1,095 pounds of fruit is as follows: 100 square feet of strawberries (100 lbs) 100 square feet of melons (200 lbs) 200 square feet of blackberries and raspberries (100 lbs) 2 sour cherries (300 lbs) 5 dwarf apple trees (800 lbs) Recognizing that the hypothetical family of three requires 750 pounds of food.

Oats yield only 10 pounds per 100 square feet, but wheat can yield as much as 20 pounds in the same region. And so, dividing 750 by 20 and multiplying by 100 provides 3,750 square feet of space for a fairly limited volume of food carbohydrates. On top of that, this small amount of grain growth is not enough to warrant having a thresher, and the grain will have to be threshed by hand — an exceedingly time-consuming process. There is also a method of converting it into grain and/or flour by mouth. Over the years, I've done a lot of that, and it's a tough job. Raising grains can become more feasible if a appropriate thresher is available at a reasonable expense, and a range of public domain prototypes are open to people who are technically skilled. Two of the most successful projects were co-created by Allen Dong and Roger Edberg; they were given to the public domain by the designers as a contribution to mankind. These sketches can be found on pages 174 and 176. Despite the fact that the USDA considers potatoes as a vegetable, a portion of the grains in the diet can be substituted and this can have beneficial effects on general health, stamina and mood. It is quick to produce three hundred and fifty pounds of potatoes in 200 square feet. Substituting that only 360 pounds of grain will still be required for a portion of the grain harvest.

Growing grain for food purposes (as opposed to cropping) in a mini-farm needs to be carefully considered from an economic point of view. In 2006, the most costly organic wheat sold for less than $15 in a 50-pound pack. Fifty pounds of the finest organic bread on the market is reportedly worth $28. It would require 300 square feet of beds to grow so much wheat, and the same amount of land will produce more than $1,400 worth of marketable crops instead.

In addition, hand threshing wheat is time-consuming and must be accompanied by grinding. Overall, it just doesn't make sense for a mini-farmer to raise grains for their food benefit in the

United States. That's why, unlike the Grow Biointensive approach, my approach to mini-farming doesn't prioritize growing grains at home. When you cultivate grains at home, you're going to need a grain grinder.

If you can find a thresher inexpensive and don't like grinding 3,800 square feet of flour, a much easier solution is to learn how to use a bread machine. Purchasing bulk flour and whole grains, using a bread machine, and studying how to produce grain-based goods from scratch at home would eventually be more economically profitable and time-consuming than growing grain for food, unless you live in a remote area where such an otherwise economically unwise method is required. Food machines have been the best trend ever since ... Bread diced. Fresh bread in the health food store typically costs $4 per loaf when it is written. By using a bread machine and ordering the ingredients in bulk, you end up with chemical-free bread costing about $0.50 per loaf.

Average Crop Yields Planted Intensively Crop

Yield in Pounds per 100 Square Feet

Green beans (as a vegetable)

100 Green beans (dried, as a protein)

20 Beets (just the roots)

200 Beets (just the greens)

200 Broccoli

75 Cabbage

300 Cauliflower

200 Carrots

350 Chard

550 Corn (on the cob)

55 Corn (dried for cornmeal)

18 Cucumber

360 Eggplant

100 Kale

120 Leeks

500 Leaf lettuce

320 Head lettuce

180 Muskmelons

100 Onions

300 Peppers

120 Peas

100 Parsnips

290 Pumpkins

120 Spinach

130 Sunflower (shelled seeds)

6 Summer squash

250 Winter squash

200 Tomatoes

250 Watermelons

180 Barley

20 Oats

10 Rye

20 Wheat

Protein is the easiest to fulfill of all food needs. Depending on your tastes, meat may need to be bought, but it is possible to grow meat and eggs at home by raising poultry. Larger animals, such as sheep and cattle, are too large to be raised cost-effectively on smaller fields. The particulars of raising small livestock will be discussed in a later chapter, so you might want to include a chicken coop in your farm program. Yet meat is not the only protein source. Dry beans, such as pinto, kidney, black turtle, soya, and others, are high in protein and easy to produce.

I sow my dried beans in the middle of my corn stalks, so they effectively take zero space. As mentioned earlier in this chapter, just half a cup of cooked dried beans is a USDA serving of beef. It's just around 1/4 cup of beans in their dry condition.

Vegetable proteins are rarely complete, meaning that they lack one or two amino acids, although this shortage can be solved by supplementing beans with grain proteins such as wheat and corn. This way, the whole mixture of essential amino acids is available. I don't climb on the vegetarian soapbox here.

What I'm suggesting now is that if you just eat dried beans and whole grain bread a few days a week, your wellbeing won't fail, so you'll save a lot of money on beef. For short, assuming that whole grains and flours are imported rather than grown at home, the basic food requirements of the household (other than meat) can be fulfilled by growing 700 square feet of vegetables and 200 square feet of potatoes or other tubers, buying flour for bulk, and growing a number of fruit trees and vines. Protein can be obtained by purchasing beef, raising livestock, and using beans and grains.

## Chapter Ten
## Selecting and saving seedin Mini-Farming

The selection of seeds can seem like an overwhelming task, especially if you are looking at a half dozen seed catalogs on a cold winter's day in January. When I look at seed catalogs, my eyes get bigger than my belly, and my mouth starts watering at each description of a different variety of each plant. Pretty soon, I have checked off enough different kinds of seeds that if I were to actually grow all of them, I would need a 600-acre farm and an impressive staff of workers. Seeds are a very compact form of material wealth. A single packet of 30 tomato seeds that costs $2 can easily produce bushels and bushels of tomatoes—enough to make salsa and spaghetti sauce for the family for a year with leftovers to sell or give away. In addition, seeds, when properly selected and saved, are an insurance policy against hard times. Anyone with limited space should be picky about seed selections in terms of climate preferences, productivity per unit area, disease resistance, and taste preferences. And if you save seed from plants grown the prior year, you will dramatically reduce the need to purchase seed.

Home-saved seeds in airtight vials. Also, raised-bed practices don't sow seeds in a row too closely together and then go back and thin out half the plants—thus wasting the seeds—as the directions on the seed packet instruct. In intensive agriculture, each seed is planted individually at the optimal spacing the first time around—so not a single seed is wasted. Thus, the seed orders placed by a mini-farmer after the second year of farming will likely be a small number of hybrid vegetables selected for a particular reason, a few plants for which saving seed

was either too difficult or unsuccessful, and a handful of new crop varieties that the farmer wants to try out. The full order for a minifarm that will feed a family of three plus generate optional replacement income will probably amount to only $100 worth of seeds plus shipping after the second year if the farmer saves seeds from annual vegetables.

Explanation of Plant Varieties

There are two terms that will be used interchangeably in the remainder of this chapter and are used periodically throughout this book that need to be understood: variety and cultivar. In the sense in which I use the terms, they have the same meaning, but to explain what I mean, I have to get into a bit of biology. Living things are categorized by biologists according to broad categories first and then into ever-finer categories. The broadest categories would be, for example, "plants" and "animals." The order of classification by plant scientists is kingdom, division, class, order, family, tribe, genus, and species. A variety is a subset of a species, and a cultivar is a cultivated variety. The actual meaning of the word species is disputed even among scientists, but the generally accepted definition is that a species is made up of a population capable of interbreeding. Typically, two plants are considered to be members of the same species if they can interbreed and produce seeds that will grow plants that will also produce seeds. Thus cabbage, cauliflower, and broccoli are all members of the same species because they can interbreed with each other. However, there are certainly significant differences between these plants! The fact that two plants are members of the same species doesn't make them identical.

If you look through a seed catalog under "broccoli," you will find anywhere from 3 to 20 different types of broccoli. The sixth edition of the Garden Seed Inventory lists 32 different open-pollinated types of broccoli. These various types of broccoli have differences in taste, color, disease resistance, vitamin content, how long they take to produce a broccoli stalk, and a host of other important characteristics. Each of the different types of broccoli is its own variety. Some food crops, like broccoli, have a very small number of varieties in existence, but others, like tomato, have over a thousand different varieties. You might select a particular variety of a given crop for any number of reasons—taste, pest resistance, short season, and so on. This is what I am referring to when I talk about a plant variety. In open-pollinated varieties, the traits that distinguish one variety from another are reliably inherited from one generation to the next. Existing plant varieties are the culmination of untold thousands of years of careful selection for various traits; new varieties are created in the same fashion all the time. Since plant characteristics are heritable, as a mini-farmer, you will have the ability to select the best-growing plants of a given variety as parents for new seeds, and over time you can end up creating your own specifically adapted plant varieties.

Selecting Plant Varieties

A mini-farmer needs four types of information to select plant varieties: local climate, available varieties, personal tastes, and plant spacing/ yields. To this basic information you will eventually add your own experiences. Local climate information can be found from the local agricultural

extension service or from the Web site of the National Climatic Weather Center. The Web site Weather.com also has a section specifically for gardens. The idea is to find out the length of the local growing season, so that plant varieties can be selected that have enough time to fully mature. A farmer in Virginia will have a much wider selection of appropriate corn and watermelon to choose from than a farmer in Vermont. Because open-pollinated varieties of crops produce seeds that can be used to grow the same crop again the next year, they are a much better choice for mini-farmers.

Seed can be saved from the most productive or hardy plants so that, over time, the open-pollinated variety that the farmer started with has been specifically adapted to that farm's climate and growing conditions. None of this is possible with interbred hybrids, which don't produce reusable seed, making open-pollinated seeds the better default choice of the farmer. The matter of hybrids has been oversimplified a bit.

Given a few years of careful selection and adequate space, it is possible with many (though not all) hybrids to convert them into a new true-totype open-pollinated variety that preserves the desired traits of the hybrid but allows for saving seeds.

There are also some cases in which hybrids provide a significant advantage over otherwise equivalent open-pollinated varieties; corn is probably the best example. The difference in productivity between hybrid and open-pollinated corn can be huge, with the hybrid producing considerably more, and when a farmer is raising food in a very small area, differences in productivity make a difference. There are also instances in which hybrid plants incorporate traits such as disease resistance, and using a hybrid variety can save the farmer from needing to use fungicides on the crops. Outside of such cases, the overwhelming preponderance of a farmer's crops should be open-pollinated. The good news about open-pollinated seeds is that they have become increasingly popular and are available from a number of companies at good prices.

An important aspect of selecting seeds is the need for experimentation. There are hundreds of varieties of peas, beans, carrots, and other crops available, and each variety will perform differently because of climatic and soil differences as well as genetic variations that affect flavor. It is good to set aside a small area just for experimenting with new crop varieties and keep careful notes of the results.

Selecting Parents

Since many important characteristics of a plant variety are hereditary, it makes sense to save seeds from plants that do best in your own environment and to avoid saving seeds from plants that do poorly. This is most reliable when dealing with self-pollinating, plants, as both the mother and the father of the seed are known.

For insect- or wind-pollinated plants, though, only the mother is known. Even so, it is better to know that at least one of the parent plants was superior. The problem of unknown parentage can be dealt with by culling inferior-performing plants before they are mature enough to pollinate or by using hand pollination to ensure that both parents are known. Either way, by selecting parentage, the farmer constantly increases the seed pool in quality and productivity.

Saving Seeds

As previously noted, one of the advantages of open-pollinated seeds is that they can be saved so that the need to purchase seeds each year is reduced. Like anything else, there are costs and benefits that the farmer has to consider, and in all likelihood you will end up saving seeds from some crops but not others. A mini-farm exists as a way to produce food rather than an exercise in seed saving. Some seeds, like tomato and pepper, can be saved with minimal effort or inconvenience while others such as cauliflower will require significant efforts and land.

If the production and sale of seeds is something you are interested in, then extraordinary efforts to save seed are worthwhile. Outside of that, if buying a packet of seed for $1.50 saves hours of effort and tying up land that would otherwise be productive, it makes sense to buy the seeds. You will need to make that determination on the basis of your own circumstances and interests. Saving seeds is a broad enough topic that entire books have been written on this subject alone. The gist, though, is straightforward: Nature mandates that plants reproduce themselves, and plants procreate by producing seeds. If these seeds are saved andreplanted, they will re-create the original plant. There are three major sets of plant attributes that affect seed saving.

The first is whether the plant is annual, biennial, or perennial. Annual plants produce seed every year and are planted newly each year. Biennial plants require two years in the ground to produce seed. Perennial plants will continue to grow from year to year but often produce seed annually. Second is whether the plant is predominantly self-pollinating or predominantly cross-pollinating. Cross-pollinators require pollen from another plant to make seed, while strongly self-pollinating plants may fertilize their own flowers before the flowers even open! This attribute exists on a continuum with beans, for example, being almost exclusively self-pollinated and corn being exclusively cross-pollinated. Finally, the actual seeds will require either dry processing or wet processing, depending on the nature of the fruit. Spinach seeds are dry like grains and will be processed differently from tomato seeds immersed in fluid. These attributes ultimately determine how much effort and land the farmer has to invest to produce seed. Biennials require overwintering and, especially north of Maryland, special attention so that they live through the winter.

Plants that are predominantly cross-pollinating require a fairly large population, sometimes as many as 400 plants, to avoid a phenomenon known as "inbreeding depression" in which seed produced from an insufficient quantity of parent plants exhibits progressively decreased vigor and productivity. Seed processing generally, whether wet or dry, can require a fair amount of time. Table 16 lists the seed-saving characteristics of a number of common crops. Saving seed from biennial plants presents difficulties for the minifarmer whose every square foot of garden bed is important, and also because plants that are wintered-over in the garden complicate crop rotation schedules and the use of cover crops.

Luckily, most biennial plants flower and set seed early in spring so they are out of the way in time for summer planting. A good compromise for farmers who wish to raise their ownbiennial seeds is to set aside one or two beds for the specific purpose of producing seed. Such beds can be protected over the winter with a hoop tunnel

Inbreeding Depression and Genetic Diversity

For those plants that are self-pollinating, the number in that column (followed by an asterisk) represents the minimum number of plants from which seed should be saved to preserve a good cross-section of the gene pool for that particular variety. These numbers represent the plant populations used in commercial seed production. If the seed is being produced for home use, there is generally little harm in reducing the population by 25% or even 50%.

## Isolation Distance

For seed production, it is important to observe the minimum isolation distances given in Table 16 . These distances are for producing seed for home use. For commercial distribution, the distances would be greater in many cases. These isolation distances specify the minimum distance that a plant has to be from another plant of the same species but a different variety to keep the two

from interbreeding and producing seeds that won't duplicate either plant. At first glance, this looks easier than it actually is for the following reason. On a farm that occupies less than a quarter acre, all of the plants are within 100 feet of each other, meaning that for purposes of seed saving, there won't be enough isolation distance available to grow more than one variety of a given species without using isolation cages or other special seed-saving techniques to prevent interbreeding. This isn't a problem with self-pollinators like peas, beans, and tomatoes but can pose a real challenge with squash, spinach, or corn.

Isolation by Time

Some brassica family plants, like broccoli, are annual while others, like cauliflower, are biennial. This means that isolation between the two can be based on timing as broccoli will have long since made its seed before cauliflower flowers the following spring. The same technique can be used if the time of flowering is different for two varieties of the same species because of differences in maturation rates.

Orchestrating this sort of isolation would be somewhat delicate but certainly possible. Another method for the farmer dedicated to saving seeds is to make use of the fact that many seeds retain their viability (ability to sprout and grow a healthy plant) for a number of years and therefore don't need to be grown for seed each year. Cucumber seeds, for example, will remain viable for at least five years if stored properly.

You could grow a different variety of cucumber each year for three years and save the seed from each variety. Then, on the fourth year, grow the same variety that you grew the first year. Thatway you are maintaining the seeds for three different varieties of cucumbers without having to do anything exotic to keep the varieties from interbreeding.

## Barrier Isolation

Barrier isolation is the practice of using a physical barrier to keep flowers from one plant from pollinating another. The two methods most practiced are alternate-day caging and hand pollination. Alternate-day caging is done by building cages out of fine window screen or floating row cover that will fit over the plants—two varieties of carrots, for example. On the first day, one variety is covered with a cage, and on the second day, the other variety is covered.

This allows insects to pollinate both without crosspollinating them. Hand pollination is easiest on plants with large flowers—like cucumbers and squash—but can be done on many other plants given a sufficiently steady hand. Hand pollination is made easy with members of the squash and cucumber family because of the fact that they grow large male and female flowers separately.

A bag is used to protect the female flower from undesirable pollen until it is hand pollinated using a male flower of the farmer's choosing. The female flower is protected with a bag again until it is no longer receptive to pollen, and that fruit is marked for seed usage. If female flowers are caught before they first open, hand pollination can be very successful at maintaining purity even in instances where multiple varieties of the same species are grown.

Dry Processing

Seeds that are naturally dry—such as those of spinach and wheat—are processed to separate the seeds from other plant materials by screening and winnowing. Screening is done with a screen selected for a mesh size that allows the seeds through but nothing larger. (Southern Exposure Seed Exchange sells screens that are presized for particular types of seeds.) This eliminates the larger debris. Debris smaller than the seeds is removed by winnowing.

Winnowing can be accomplished by pouring the seeds from one container to another in front of a stiff breeze or a fan. Lighter materials get blown away, and seeds get preserved. (Getting good at this takes practice!) Some dry seeds require threshing to be saved in appreciable quantities. Threshing is a technique that uses physical force to break away the pods surrounding the seeds and can be accomplished in a number of creative ways.

Traditionally, farmers used a flail resembling a set of nunchakus for this task. The plants requiring threshing would be placed in a sturdy sack, and then the sack would be beaten with the flail and all the seeds would end up in the bottom of the bag. Another common technique is to place the plants to be threshed on a tarp, put another tarp on top so the plants are sandwiched in between, and then walk around on them. Melons, winter squash, and green peppers are wet fruit, but their seeds can be saved like dry seeds by washing them in water to remove any traces of pulp and then drying before storage.

Wet Processing

For plants whose seeds are embedded in damp flesh, studies have shown that the viability of the seeds is highest if the fruit is allowed to become a bit more than fully ripe before harvesting. Such wet seeds will also benefit from fermentation processing. In fermentation processing, the seeds and pulp are scraped into a glass container—a clean pint jar for example—and about half that volume of tap water is added to the jar. Swirl and mix, then cover the container and put it in a warm place. Three days later, the contents of the container have grown a rather disgusting mold, and the good seeds have sunk to the bottom. The seeds that have sunk to the bottom are removed, washed, and dried. Fermentation is not strictly necessary, but studies indicate that this sort of processing mimics natural processes and has been demonstrated to reduce the incidence of diseases in the seeds.

Storing Seeds

The length of time that seeds are viable depends on how you store them, and this applies to both purchased seeds and homegrown seeds. The two most important factors affecting the longevity of seeds are heat and moisture. Studies have demonstrated that between the temperatures of 32 degrees F and 112 degrees F, the time that a seed is viable doubles for every 9 degrees F that the temperature is lowered.41 The moisture content of the seeds is also important, as similar studies have shown that an increase in seed moisture of as little as 5% to 10% can reduce seed viability more rapidly than increasing the temperature from 68 degrees F to 104 degrees F. 42 (Seed banks store seeds in chest freezers at below-freezing temperatures. For home seed savers, storing seeds at temperatures below freezing is unusual because the moisture level of the seed must be carefully controlled to keep such cold temperatures from damaging the seed.)

Seed Characteristics

Tools for properly drying seeds for storage. Therefore, keep seeds cool and dry. This is easy to accomplish using moisture-indicating silica gel, small muslin bags like those used for spices, and mason jars with sealing tops. Moistureindicating silica gel and the small muslin bags can be purchased from the Southern Exposure Seed Exchange. When dry, moistureindicating silica gel is blue, and when damp it is pink. Once it becomes pink, put it on some aluminum foil on a pan in the oven on the lowest setting and gently heat it until it turns uniformly blueagain. It can be reused indefinitely, so it's a good investment.

Place the seeds to be stored in a mason jar either within paper seed packets or not, because the seed packets pass moisture readily. (You might do this with commercial seed packets you received in the mail, just to make sure they are properly dehydrated before storage.) Put two or three tablespoons of moisture-indicating silica gel in a drawstring muslin bag and put it in the jar with the seeds and seal.

A week later, remove the bag containing silica gel from the jar, reseal, and place the jar in a cool basement or a refrigerator. If you use this method, your seeds should remain viable for a long time, and your investment in either purchased seeds or the personal effort of saving seeds is protected.

www.ingramcontent.com/pod-product-compliance
Lightning Source LLC
Chambersburg PA
CBHW070907080526
44589CB00013B/1211